LEARNER'S
POCKET

# Verbs and Tenses

Jon Hird

OXFORD
UNIVERSITY PRESS

# OXFORD
### UNIVERSITY PRESS

Great Clarendon Street, Oxford, OX2 6DP, United Kingdom

Oxford University Press is a department of the University of
Oxford. It furthers the University's objective of excellence
in research, scholarship, and education by publishing
worldwide. Oxford is a registered trade mark of Oxford
University Press in the UK and in certain other countries

ISBN: 978 0 19 432569 1

Printed in China

This book is printed on paper from certified and well-
managed sources

Index by Fiona Barr

# Contents

CONTENTS

## Modal verbs

## Uses of major verbs

# Introduction

*Oxford Learner's Pocket Verbs and Tenses* provides a user-friendly and concise explanation of a key element of the English language: verbs and tenses. It is ideal for learners at Intermediate level and above.

The book comprises 110 units, divided into 14 sections. Each unit takes a key topic relating to verbs and tenses and clearly explains form, meaning, and use. A useful tip is included in each unit, often featuring idiomatic use of the verbs and tenses covered. The book includes a great many illustrative example sentences, which cover both spoken and written English. It also warns of common errors to avoid.

The content of the units reflects thorough corpus-based research into current use of verbs and tenses. Extensive cross-referencing allows learners to build a full understanding of the connections between different topics.

Following the units is a glossary, which explains all the grammar terms used. This is followed by appendices, which include information on verb formation, a guide to spelling, and comprehensive verb lists. Finally, a full index is included to help with navigation.

*Oxford Learner's Pocket Verbs and Tenses* is ideal for students in schools and colleges as well as independent adult learners. The pocket size of the book means it can be carried or kept anywhere and used for instant reference. It is ideal for exam preparation and revision, and has been written with the syllabuses of IELTS, PET, FCE, CAE, and CPE in mind. It corresponds to CEF levels B1, B2, C1, and C2. It will complement any English course by offering a deeper explanation of verbs and tenses.

This book may be used alongside *Oxford Learner's Pocket Grammar, Oxford Learner's Pocket Dictionary, Oxford Learner's Pocket Word Skills,* and *Oxford Learner's Pocket Phrasal Verbs and Idioms.* Together, these books offer a complete, pocket-sized English language reference package.

*A note on cross-references*

Cross-references use the symbol ▶. Most cross-references are to unit numbers, e.g. ▶ 2 is a cross-reference to Unit 2. Some cross-references are to pages within the Appendices, and here the page number is given, e.g. ▶ page 329.

# 1 Intransitive, transitive, and linking verbs

**A** There are three basic verb types: intransitive verbs, transitive verbs, and linking verbs.

- Intransitive verbs do not have an object.

  Patrick **has arrived**.

  It**'s raining**.

  He **died** in 2005.

  I **went** to London yesterday.

- Transitive verbs must have an object.

  I**'ve bought a guitar**.

  He never **wears jeans**.

  I **made a mistake**.

  I **found a wallet** in the street.

  For verbs with two objects ▶ 2.

- Linking verbs have a complement which tells us something about the subject, such as what it is, how it feels, or what it is like. A complement can be an adjective or adjective phrase, a noun or noun phrase, a prepositional phrase, or a clause.

  I **feel cold**.

  She **seems very friendly**.

  The event **was a great success**.

  The lift **is out of order**.

  The film **wasn't what I expected**.

**B** Some verbs can be of more than one type depending on how we use them.

> *Have you eaten?* (intransitive)
> *Who's eaten the cake?* (transitive)
> *We got lost for a while.* (linking)
> *I got €50 from the ATM.* (transitive)

**C** Some transitive verbs have an object which itself has a complement.

> *The publicity **made the film a massive worldwide hit**.*
> *The judge **found all the defendants guilty**.*
> *The housework **kept us busy all day**.*
> *It **drives me mad**!*

## Verb + adverbial

**D** We use adverbials (*for a while, from the ATM, yesterday, in London*, etc.) with all the verb types. This can be just verb + adverbial or in combination with an object or complement.

> *We **waited for an hour**.*
> *I **saw Erica in London yesterday**.*
> *I **was tired all morning**.*
> *The lift **was out of order last week**.*

### TIP

When we use an adverbial, it most commonly goes after the object or complement.
*We bought a new TV **yesterday**.*
*I was hungry **all day**.*
*The housework kept us busy **for hours**.*

# 2 Verbs with two objects

A Some transitive verbs can have two objects, an indirect object and a direct object. These verbs are generally those which express giving, conveying, or telling something to somebody.

The indirect object is usually a person (*I gave **Tania** a book*) and the direct object is usually a thing (*I gave Tania **a book***).

When a verb has two objects, there are usually two possible structures.

- One structure is verb + indirect object + direct object.
   *We bought **Julia a watch**.*
   *Show **Alex the photo**.*
   *Shall I get **Suzy a ticket**?*
   *I made **my mum a cake**.*

- The other structure is verb + direct object + *to/for* + indirect object.
   *We bought **a watch for Julia**.*
   *Show **the photo to Alex**.*
   *Shall I get **a ticket for Suzy**?*
   *I made **a cake for my mum**.*

When both objects are a noun or noun phrase, we can generally use either structure.

## Pronouns as the object

B  When both the direct object and the indirect object are pronouns, again we can generally use either structure.
> *Ulrich bought **me it**.*
> OR *Ulrich bought **it for me**.*

But, when only one of the objects is a pronoun, the pronoun usually goes first. Therefore, if the direct object is a pronoun, we use the structure with *to/for*.
> *I'll give **it to Andrew**.*
> NOT ~~I'll give Andrew it.~~

If the indirect object is a pronoun, we generally use the structure without *to/for*.
> *I'll send **you the photos**.*

## Multi-syllable verbs

C  With some multi-syllable verbs that have two objects we only usually use the structure with *to/for*.
> *He **explained the rules to me**.*
> NOT ~~He explained me the rules.~~
> *They **donated millions to the charity**.*
> NOT ~~They donated the charity millions.~~

Such verbs include: *announce, communicate, deliver, demonstrate, describe, introduce, mention, obtain, propose, repeat, report, suggest.*

## 2 *To* or *for*

**D** Verbs which use *for* include: *buy, book, choose, cook, fetch, find, fix, get, make, order, pick, reserve, save.*

> Dave **bought** it **for** me.

Verbs which use *to* include: *award, bring, fax, feed, donate, email, give, hand, leave* (in a will), *lend, offer, owe, pass, pay, post, read, sell, send, show, take, teach, tell, text, throw, write.*

> I'll **email** the photo **to** you.

### Passive verbs

**E** When a verb with two objects is used in the passive, there are two possible structures.

Active:

> The jury awarded **first prize to Katie**.

Passive:

> **Katie** was awarded **first prize**.
> **First prize** was awarded **to Katie**.

In the passive, the structure that has the person at the beginning (**Katie** *was awarded* …) is more common, especially in more informal contexts.

---

**TIP**

In informal spoken English, when the verb has two pronouns, you may hear the direct pronoun before the indirect pronoun without *to/for*.

Ana gave **it me**. OR Ana gave **me it**.

---

# 3 Auxiliary verbs

A  Auxiliary verbs combine with other verbs to form tenses, questions, negatives, and passives. There are three auxiliary verbs in English: *do*, *be*, and *have*.

## Do, be, and have

B  We most commonly use *do* (*do*, *does*, *did*) to make questions and negatives in the present simple and past simple tenses.
   Where **do** you live?
   I **don't** agree.
   **Did** you go out last night?
   I **didn't** have lunch today.

C  We use *be* (*am*, *is*, *are*, *was*, *were*) to form a continuous tense ▸ 11, 18 and to form the passive ▸ 38–43.
   It**'s** snowing.
   What **were** you doing?
   Where **were** the last Olympics held?

D  We use *have* (*have*, *has*, *had*) to form a perfect tense.
   Sonia**'s** gone to the supermarket.
   I **haven't** finished.
   We**'d** met before.

   We also use *have* to form a causative statement (when you cause or arrange for something to happen) ▸ 40.
   We**'re having** the house decorated.

## 3 Auxiliary verbs in questions

E All three auxiliary verbs are used in forming questions. In questions the auxiliary verb goes before the subject.

> Where **do you** work?
> **Is it** raining?
> **Have you** been to the US?

For more on questions ▶ 4–8.

## Short responses

F We use auxiliary verbs in short responses to yes/no questions.

> Are you going home? ~ Yes, I **am**.
> Did you see Alice? ~ Yes, I **did**.
> Have you had lunch? ~ Yes, we **have**.

We use them in responses with *so* and *neither*.

> I'm starving. ~ So **am** I.
> We went away for the weekend. ~ So **did** we.
> I haven't seen Janice for ages. ~ Neither **have** I.

We use them in echo questions.

> It's raining. ~ **Is** it?
> We saw Harry last night. ~ **Did** you?
> How is he?
> Danny's sold his car. ~ He's **done** what?

For more on echo questions ▶ 6.

## Question tags

3

G We use auxiliary verbs in question tags.
> *Jim's in Berlin, **isn't** he?*
> *He writes novels, **doesn't** he?*
> *You haven't seen my mobile, **have** you?*
> *You'll be at the conference, **won't** you?*
> *James didn't go, **did** he?*

For more on question tags ▶ 8.

## Emphasis

H We can use the auxiliary verb *do* to give emphasis to a statement in the present or past simple. In speaking, we stress *do*.
> *I **do** like Thai food.*
> *I **did** enjoy that film.*
> *He doesn't watch much TV, but he **does** like nature programmes.*

With tenses and forms that already have an auxiliary verb, we stress the auxiliary to express emphasis.
> *I **am** looking forward to the weekend.*

### TIP

We also use modal verbs as auxiliary verbs in the ways described above
▶ 73–85.
*Can you speak French? ~ No, I **can't**.*
*You couldn't help me, **could** you?*

# 4 Questions

## Auxiliaries and modals

A  We form questions by putting an auxiliary verb before the subject.

   For the present and past simple we use the auxiliary verb *do*.
   ***Do you*** know Sue Smith?
   ***Did Jack*** phone this morning?

   Continuous and perfect tenses already include the auxiliary verbs *be* or *have*.
   ***Are you*** doing anything at the weekend?
   ***Was the internet*** working earlier?
   ***Have you*** seen Karen recently?
   ***Has Joe*** been waiting long?

B  For the present and past simple of *be* as a main verb, we do not use an auxiliary verb. We put *be* before the subject.
   ***Is she*** OK?
   ***Are you*** ready?
   ***Were they*** late?
   NOT *Does she be OK?*
   NOT *Did they be late?*

C  With modal verbs we put the modal verb before the subject.
   ***Can you*** help me please?
   ***Must you*** leave already?
   ***Will Lisa*** be at the meeting?
   NOT *Do you can help me?*

## Question words/phrases

D  We generally put question words
(*what, where,* etc.) and question
phrases (*what time, how much,* etc.)
at the beginning of a question.

> **Which** do you prefer?
> **What** did you do at the weekend?
> **Where**'s Olga going?
> **When** was the first World Cup?
> **How much** was lunch?

## Intonation

E  The intonation in a question that has
a question word (sometimes called a
'wh-question') goes down at the end of
the question.

> *Which is Helena's car?* ↘
> *How far is it to Curitiba?* ↘

The intonation in a question that
doesn't have a question word
(sometimes called a 'yes/no question')
goes up at the end of the question.

> *Is this Helena's car?* ↗
> *Is it far to Curitiba?* ↗

## Subject questions

F  When we are asking for information
about the subject of a sentence,
the word order is the same as in a
statement. The question word or
question phrase replaces the subject.

> **Who** teaches you English?
> (Ms Judd teaches us English.)

4

***Which*** countries border Tunisia?
(Algeria and Libya border Tunisia.)
***What*** caused the problem?
***What***'s making that noise?
***Who*** last used the computer?

In subject questions, we do not use
the auxiliary verb *do* for the present
and past simple tenses.

NOT ~~Who does teach you English?~~
NOT ~~What did cause the problem?~~

However, we do use the forms *doesn't*,
*don't*, or *didn't* to ask about negative
ideas.

***Who doesn't*** want any tea?
***Who didn't*** go to the meeting?
***Which*** lights ***don't*** work?

### TIP

You may hear *does* pronounced as *'s*
in some questions in informal spoken
English.
*'Who**'s** this bag belong to?'*
*'What**'s** it look like?'*
*'Where**'s** he live?'*
*'How long**'s** the film last?'*
Note this contraction is not used in
written English.

# 5 Negative questions

**A** We make a negative question by adding *-n't* to the auxiliary verb. We do not use the full form *not*.

*Isn't Diana here?*
*Don't you like Indian food?*
*Haven't we met before?*
*Why didn't you get a taxi?*
NOT ~~Is not Diana here?~~

However, we can sometimes use *not* after the subject.

*Is Diana **not** here?*
*Are you **not** coming with us?*

The negative of *am I* is *aren't I*. However, we can also use *am I not*.

***Aren't I** coming with you?*
***Am I not** coming with you?*

## Negative question without a question word

**B** We use a negative question without a question word (*what*, *why*, etc.) in two main ways:

• to show surprise or when something is not as expected

***Don't** you like football? I thought you did.*
***Haven't** you left yet? You'd better get a move on.*
***Wasn't** the conference useful?*
***Doesn't** Sam play the guitar? I was sure he did.*

13

- as a real question, but when you expect or hope the listener will agree

  **Haven't** we met before? Istanbul, wasn't it?

  **Aren't** you a friend of Marco's?

  **Isn't** it a lovely day?

  **Doesn't** Sam play the guitar? He plays jazz, doesn't he?

## Negative question with a question word

C We use a negative question with a question word to ask for information.

  **What don't** you like about your job?

  **Why didn't** you wait for us?

  **Why isn't** Abril coming with us?

  **Who hasn't** got a drink?

  **Which** café **doesn't** Suzy want to go to?

## Yes and no answers

D The answer *no* to a negative question generally means that the opposite is true, and *yes* means that the suggestion in the question is correct.

  *Didn't you go away at the weekend?* ~ **No**, we stayed at home. / **Yes**, we went to Brighton.

  *You haven't eaten all day. Aren't you hungry?* ~ **No**, I'm fine. / **Yes**, I'm starving actually.

However, if the questioner expects agreement, we can use *no* to agree.

*Don't you like football? ~ **No**, I hate it.*
*Doesn't the light work? ~ **No**, I think the bulb's gone.*

## Negative words

E We can use other negative words such as *no*, *no one*, and *never* to form negative questions.

*Is there **no** sugar?*
*Why is there **no one** here?*
*Did **nobody** tell you about the meeting?*
*Have you **never** met Jo?*

---

### TIP

*Why don't we/you* and *why doesn't he/she* are useful expressions for making suggestions.

***Why don't we** get a taxi?*
***Why don't you** look for another job?*
***Why doesn't he** talk to his boss?*

We can also use *why not* as an alternative to *why don't we/you.*

***Why not** look for another job?*
***Why not** get a taxi?*

---

## ✎ 6 Echo questions

A An echo question is when we ask
a question in direct response to
something we have just heard. This
is usually to express surprise and/or
to ask for clarification. There are four
typical structures:
*She's going where?*
*You did what?*
*Did you?*
*He's getting married?*

The intonation of echo questions
is very important and in all echo
questions the intonation rises
(*You're doing what? ↗ Did you? ↗*).
In general, the greater the rise in the
voice, the greater the surprise.

### *She's going where?* etc.

B We can replace the information we are
questioning with a question word.
*Olga's going to Siberia. ~ She's going*
***where?***
*It was £85. ~ It was* ***how much?***
*Your flight's at 11.30 on Friday. ~ It's*
***when*** *on Friday?*

### *You did what?* etc.

C For actions, we can replace a whole
verb phrase with the correct form of
*do + what*. This is usually when we
want to show disbelief.

*I told Jenny everything.* ~ *You **did what**?*
*Ken's sold his house.* ~ *He's **done what**?*

### *Did you?* etc.

D We can use an auxiliary verb (*be*, *do*, *have*, or modal) + pronoun. Note that for the present and past simple, we use the auxiliary verb *do*. We sometimes call this kind of response an 'echo tag'.
*They live in Oxford.* ~ ***Do they?***
*I saw Petra last night.* ~ ***Did you?***
*I can't drive.* ~ ***Can't you?***
*Fred isn't coming with us.* ~ ***Isn't he?***

Rising intonation (*Did you?* ↗) shows that we are surprised by and/or interested in what was said. Falling intonation (*Did you?* ↘) suggests that we are not surprised or not interested.

### *He's getting married?* etc.

E We can repeat the information.
*Juan's getting married.* ~ ***He's getting married?***
*Sorry we're late. We got lost.* ~ ***You got lost?***

### TIP

Note that while it is considered grammatically correct to use *whom* as the object of a verb, in spoken English it is very common and acceptable to use *who*.
*I saw Vera last night.* ~ *You saw **who/whom**?*

# 7 Indirect questions

**A** We use indirect questions to be more tentative. This is usually either:

- to sound more polite or formal
  *Do you know where the nearest ATM is?*

- or because the question is sensitive or personal
  *Do you know if Jen's got a boyfriend?*
  *I was wondering if you knew anything about the Harrison merger?*

**B** Indirect questions begin with a question phrase. Common question phrases include *could/can you tell me …?*, *I'd like to know …?*, *do you know …?*, *do you happen to know …?*, *have you any idea …?*, *I was wondering …?*, *do you mind if I ask you …?*
  **Could you tell me** where the canteen is?
  **Do you know** which is Marta's desk?
  **Have you any idea** what time it is?

The question phrase is followed by a question word or *if*. We use *if* for a question that requires a 'yes' or 'no' answer.
  *Have you any idea **where** Harry is?*
  *Do you know **if** it's going to rain later?*

We can also sometimes use *whether (or not)* instead of *if*.

*Do you know **whether or not** it's going to rain later?*

The word order after the question word or *if/whether* is the same as in a statement. We do not put the verb before the subject and we do not use the auxiliary verb *do*.

*Could you tell me **where meeting room 4 is**?*

*Do you know **if Ferhat speaks English**?*

NOT *Could you tell me where is meeting room 4?*

NOT *Do you know if Ferhat does speak English?*

C   We can also use question phrase + question word + to-infinitive.

*Do you know how **to get** to the station?*

D   We can also use question phrase + object.

*Do you know **the new PA's name**?*

We do not use *I was wondering …?* in this way.

NOT *I was wondering the new PA's name?*

### TIP

We use *would you say …?* and *do you think …?* to ask for an opinion.
***Would you say** you are a good learner?*
***Do you think** we ought to book in advance?*

# ∞ 8 Question tags

**A** We use a question tag after a statement.
We use question tags to invite or
prompt the listener to respond.

*She's from Peru, **isn't she?** ~ Yes, I
think she is.*

*It's not snowing again, **is it?** ~ I'm
afraid it is.*

## Form

**B** We form a question tag using an
auxiliary verb (*be, do, have,* or modal)
+ pronoun. We use the same auxiliary
verb as in the preceding statement.
For the present and past simple, we
use the auxiliary verb *do.*

*The bus **hasn't** left, **has it?***
*You **speak** Spanish, **don't you?***
*Kate **designed** that poster, **didn't she?***
*Olga **can** speak Polish, **can't she?***

We also use the subject *there* in a
question tag.

*There's a bus at six, **isn't there?***

If the main verb in the preceding
statement is *be,* we use *be* in the
question tag.

*Adele **is** British, **isn't she?***
*They **were** late, **weren't they?***

We use a negative question tag after
an affirmative statement.

*He's Canadian, **isn't he?***
*Dino **works** for the UN, **doesn't he?***

We use an affirmative question tag after a negative statement.

*Your flight **wasn't** too delayed, **was it**?*
*Alicia **hasn't** phoned, **has she**?*

Note the following question tag forms.

- After *I'm* or *I am* ..., we use *aren't I*?
  *I'm invited too, **aren't I**?*

- After *Let's* ..., we use *shall we*?
  *Let's go, **shall we**?*

- After subjects ending in *-one* or *-body*, we use *they* in the question tag.
  *Somebody told you, **didn't they**?*

- After subjects ending in *-thing*, we use *it* in the question tag.
  *Something is wrong, **isn't it**?*

## Intonation and use

C We use question tags with either falling or rising intonation. The intonation indicates the nature of what we say.

- We use a question tag with falling intonation when we expect the listener to agree with us.
  *It's a lovely day, isn't it?* ↘
  *You haven't been to Japan, have you?* ↘

- We use a question tag with rising intonation when we ask a real question.
  *It's the 13th today, isn't it?* ↗
  *The train takes two hours, doesn't it?* ↗

∞

We also use a question tag
with rising intonation to ask
for information or to request
something.

*You couldn't lend me €20, could
you?* ↗
*You don't know Jo's email address,
do you?* ↗

We also use a question tag
with rising intonation to show
disapproval or disbelief.

*You haven't bought yet another
new dress, have you?* ↗

## Affirmative statement + affirmative tag

D We can use an affirmative statement +
affirmative tag to check or clarify
something.

*Tania doesn't work here anymore. ~
Oh, she's **left, has she?***
*Gary didn't get here until 9.30. ~
I see. He **was** late again, **was he?***

### TIP

You may hear people using the question
tag *innit?* (a form of *isn't it?*). Many
people consider this to be incorrect
English, but it is quite common,
especially in informal speech.
*It's a great film, **innit?***

Some people also use it irrespective of
the tense and subject of the preceding
statement.
*Kris's coming with us, **innit?***

# 9 The present simple with *be* 🔄

This unit covers the form of the verb *be*. For uses of *be* ▶ 86.

A The present simple of *be* is:

I *am*    you/we/they *are*    he/she/it *is*.
I *am* a student.
We *are* French. Ulrich *is* German.
My parents *are* teachers.

However, in most cases, especially in speaking and informal writing, we use the short forms:

I*'m*    you/we/they*'re*    he/she/it*'s*.
I*'m* from London and Sam*'s* from Oxford.
Oxford*'s* a small city. It*'s* 50 miles from London.
Thanks for the coffee. ~ You*'re* welcome.
The bank*'s* on James Street.

B To form the negative we add *not* or the short form *-n't*. We do not use the auxiliary verb *do*.

I*'m* **not** hungry.
It*'s* **not** expensive.
Mr Thomas *isn't* here.
NOT ~~I don't be hungry.~~
NOT ~~It doesn't be expensive.~~

Note that the following contracted forms are both usually possible.

*We're* **not** *ready.*
OR *We* **aren't** *ready.*
*David* **isn't** *here.*
OR *David's* **not** *here.*

But we always use *I'm not* or *I am not*. We do not use ~~I amn't~~.

*I'm* **not** *tired.*
NOT ~~I amn't tired.~~

We can use the full forms *am/is/are* + *not* in more formal contexts and for emphasis.

*We* **are not** *happy with the service.*
*The meeting room* **is not** *available today.*

C To form a question we put *be* before the subject. We do not use the auxiliary verb *do*.

**Are you** *hungry?*
*What time* **is it***?*
*Where* **are my keys***?*
**Am I** *late?*
NOT ~~Do you be hungry?~~

---

### TIP

Note that in English the verb *be* may be used where a different verb is used in your language ▶ 86.
*I'm* twenty-three.
*We're* thirsty.
*She's* hungry.
*I'm* hot.

---

# 10 The present simple

## Form

A The present simple is the base form
of the verb. The third person singular
(*he/she/it*) ends in *-s*.

> I **work** in Oxford. I usually **drive** to
> work.
> My wife **works** in town. She **walks** to
> work.
> Jim **goes** to Brighton University. He
> **studies** art.

For when to use *-es* and *-ies* as the third
person singular ending ▶ page 331.

B The negative is *don't* + base form.
For the third person singular we use
*doesn't* + base form.

> I **don't understand**.
> My parents **don't speak** English.
> He **doesn't understand**.
> Carla **doesn't eat** meat or fish.

We can use the full forms *do not* and
*does not* in more formal contexts and
for emphasis.

> I **do not** accept the situation.
> She **does not** want to see him.

C In questions we use *do* + base form.
For the third person singular we use
*does* + base form.

> **Do** you **understand**?
> Where **do** you **live**?

> *Does he **understand**?*
> *When **does** the bus **leave**?*

For more about question forms ▶ 4–8.

## Use

D We use the present simple to talk about something we see as permanent or unchanging. This includes:

* facts and permanent situations
  *Water **boils** at 100°C.*
  *I **live** in Rome.*
  *The journey **takes** two hours by car.*
  *Michel **doesn't speak** English.*

* states of mind, such as thoughts, opinions, feelings, and likes/dislikes
  *I **think** he's Spanish.*
  *I **hope** it doesn't rain.*
  *I **don't like** coffee.*

* habits and routines
  *I generally **walk** to work.*
  *We usually **have** lunch at 12.30.*
  *Sam **plays** football every Thursday.*

---

### TIP

We often use frequency expressions such as *always, often, usually, generally, sometimes, hardly ever, never, every day, once a week, every Saturday, twice a year*, etc. with the present simple when we talk about habits and routines.
*I **hardly ever** play computer games.*
*I go for a run **twice a week**.*
*We **generally** get together **every Saturday**.*

# 11 The present continuous

## Form

**A** The present continuous is the present of *be* + ing-form.

> *I'm watching TV.*
> *It's raining.*
> *They're waiting for us.*

For spelling of the ing-form ▶ page 332.

**B** To form the negative we add *not* or *-n't* after *be*. There is little difference in the two forms and it is often down to personal choice.

> *They're not waiting for us.*
> OR *They aren't waiting for us.*
> *The internet's not working.*
> OR *The internet isn't working.*

We can also use the full form of *be* and *not*. This is usually in more formal contexts or for emphasis.

> *We are not expecting any problems.*

For more detail on the form and use of the negative of *be* ▶ 9, 86.

**C** To form a question we put *be* before the subject.

> *Is it raining?*
> *Are they waiting for us?*
> *Where are you going?*
> *What is Julia wearing?*

## 11 Use

**D** We use the present continuous to say that something is in progress (or not in progress) at the time of speaking. We usually see the action or situation as temporary or unfinished. This can be:

- things in progress now
  *It's **raining**.*
  *Karen **isn't wearing** her new coat.*
  *Anna and Vera **are waiting** for us.*
  *What **are** you **doing**? ~ I'm **sending** some emails.*

- things in progress around now, but not necessarily at this exact moment
  *Diana's **having** driving lessons.*
  *Is anyone **sitting** here? ~ No it's free.*
  *Are you **reading** a good book at the moment?*

- changing situations
  *Your English **is getting** better.*
  *The earth **is becoming** warmer.*
  *Unemployment **is increasing**.*

- to show we see a situation as temporary and possibly short-lived
  *I'm **working** at home this week because they're **decorating** the office.*
  *I'm **going** to the gym a lot these days.*

**E** We often use time expressions such as *now*, *right now*, *at the moment*, *at present*, *these days*, and *nowadays* with the present continuous.

*I'm* really **enjoying** work **these days**.
*I'm* **reading** a great book **at the moment**.
*Can I call you back? We're* **having**
*dinner* **right now**.

We often use *still* to show that the
action or situation continues, or *not*
+ *any more* to show that the action or
situation doesn't continue.

*We're* **still waiting** for the taxi.
*Is it* **still snowing**?
*I'm* **not having** guitar lessons **any more**.

F There are some verbs that we rarely
use in the continuous form. These are
usually verbs that describe states ▸ 21.

*It* **depends** on the weather.
*Who* **owns** this house?
NOT *It's depending on the weather.*
NOT *Who's owning this house?*

G We also use the present continuous to
talk about the future ▸ 25.

---

**TIP**

We can use the present continuous with
words such as *always*, *constantly*, and
*forever* to show that we are annoyed
by someone's repeated actions or
behaviour.
*My sister's* **always borrowing** my clothes
*without asking*.
*I'm* **forever losing** my door key.

---

# 12 The present simple or present continuous?

## Basic difference

A We use the present simple to talk about things we see as permanent, such as facts, habits, and routines.

*Steve **works** in Manchester.*
*I **don't speak** Italian.*
*It **rains** a lot at this time of year.*
*I **read** the newspaper every day.*

B We use the present continuous to talk about something which is in progress (or not in progress) at or around the time of speaking. We usually see the action or situation as temporary or unfinished.

*Harry's **working** at home this week.*
*She's **speaking** Italian with Mario.*
*It **isn't raining**. Let's go for a walk.*
*I'm **reading** a great book at the moment.*

C The following sentences illustrate the contrast between the two tenses when talking about permanent and temporary situations.

*I usually **listen** to rock music, but I'm **listening** to a lot of jazz at the moment.*
*I **work** in London, but I'm **working** in the Cambridge office this month.*

## Repeated actions

D  To talk in a neutral way about things
   that happen regularly or repeatedly, we
   usually use the present simple.

   *My computer **crashes** a lot.*
   *Fred **has** a lot of time off work.*

   However, to emphasize the
   repetitiveness of the action and/or to
   express annoyance and irritation we
   can use the present continuous with
   adverbs of frequency such as *always*,
   *forever*, and *constantly*.

   *My computer **is constantly crashing**.*
   *Fred's **always having** time off work.*

## States

E  We generally use the present simple
   to talk about states such as qualities,
   possession, and appearance, and
   mental states such as thoughts, desires,
   and feelings ▶ 21.

   *It **costs** £300.*
   *The restaurant **looks** expensive.*
   *The children **are** normally very well
   behaved.*
   *I **love** Italian food.*

   However, to add emphasis and/or to
   show that something is at a particular
   time and temporary, rather than
   a permanent attitude or situation,
   we sometimes use the present
   continuous. We often use a time

adverbial (e.g. *at the moment*, *today*) to show that the state is temporary.

*I'm really **enjoying** this pizza.*
*The weather **is looking** better this morning.*
*The children **are being** very naughty today.*

## Narrative present

F We can use both the present simple and the present continuous to make past events come to life and appear more immediate and more vivid.

*Can you believe it? I'm **sitting** on the train on my way to London last week and this girl **sits** down next to me and it's my old friend from school, Jilly.*

We can also use both present tenses to explain the plot of a story.

*An old lady **offers** to buy the child, who at the time **is living** in an orphanage.*

G We can also use the present simple and the present continuous to talk about the future ▶ 25.

---

### TIP

We can use either the present simple or the present continuous in the expression *look forward to*. The present simple is more formal and the present continuous is more informal and friendly.

*I **look forward to** meeting you.*
*I'm **looking forward to** seeing you.*

---

# 13 The imperative

## Form

A The imperative is the base form of the verb.

*Wait* for me!
*Turn* right at the traffic lights.
*Be* careful.
*Calm* down!

B To form the negative, we use *don't* + base form.

*Don't worry* about it.
*Don't be* late.
*Don't forget* to get some bread.

We can use *do not* + base form in more formal situations.

This email is automated. **Do not reply**.
Please **do not** walk on the grass.

C We use *do (not)* + base form to add emphasis.

*Do ask* if you need any help.
*Do be* quiet!
*Do not say* anything to anyone!

## Use

D We use the imperative to tell someone to do, or not to do, something. This could be:

• orders and instructions
*Restart* the computer. *Mix* the flour and water. *Don't touch*!

- signs and notices
  ***Keep*** to the left. ***Do not feed*** the animals. ***Do not use*** the towpath when flooded.

- advice, suggestions, reminders, and warnings
  ***Be*** careful. ***Try*** again. ***Don't be*** late. ***Look out!***

- informal offers, invitations, and requests
  ***Have*** a biscuit. ***Come*** with us if you like.

- good wishes
  ***Enjoy*** the party. ***Have*** a nice day.

## Always, never, and don't ever + imperative

E   We can use *always*, *never*, and *don't ever* to emphasize that the instruction or advice is permanent.
  ***Always*** try your best.
  ***Never*** open spam emails.
  ***Don't ever*** do that again.

## Subject + imperative

F   We can sometimes use subject + imperative to emphasize the role of the person or people we are addressing.
  ***You*** tell him.
  ***All of you*** listen for a moment.
  ***Everyone*** meet here at 5.30.
  ***No one*** say anything about the party.

## Imperative + question tag

G  We use imperative + *will/would/can/ could you?* to make the imperative less abrupt.

> **Wait** a minute, **will you?**
> **Give** me a hand, **could you?**
> **Pass** me the sugar, **would you?**

We use imperative + *can't you?* to express annoyance or impatience.
> **Be** quiet, **can't you?**

We use imperative + *will/won't you?* in reminders and warnings.
> **Don't forget** the milk, **will you?**
> **Drive** carefully, **won't you?**

### Will/Would you ...?

H  We can also use *will/would you ...?* in a question structure to make an imperative less direct.
> **Will you wait** here a moment?
> **Would you pass** me the water, please?

---

**TIP**

There are a number of useful expressions using the imperative.
*Calm down! Look out! Be careful!
Hurry up! Don't worry! Cheer up!
Have fun! Be quiet! Don't be silly!
Don't be nosy!*

# 14 The past simple

## Form

**A** With most verbs, we add *-ed* to the base form. These are called 'regular verbs'.

> *I **walked** to work this morning.*
> *We **watched** TV last night.*
> *Manchester City **played** Arsenal at the weekend.*

For exceptions to spelling (*studied*, *stopped*, etc.) ▶ page 331.

Some verbs have an irregular past simple form. These are called 'irregular verbs' ▶ page 329.

> *I **went** to the supermarket this morning.*
> *I **saw** James yesterday.*
> *Arsenal **lost** 2–0.*

**B** The negative is *didn't* + base form.

> *I **didn't watch** TV last night.*
> *I **didn't have** lunch today.*
> *Oliver **didn't go** out at the weekend.*
> NOT *I didn't watched TV last night.*

We can use the full form *did not* in more formal contexts and for emphasis.

> *I'm afraid we **did not receive** your booking form.*
> *I **did not eat** your chocolate!*

**C** In questions we use *did* + base form.
   ***Did*** you ***watch*** TV last night?
   *What **did** she **study** at university?*
   *What time **did** they **leave**?*
   NOT *Did you watched TV last night?*

For more about question forms ▶ 4–8.

## *Be*

**D** The verb *be* is the only exception to the rules above.

The past simple of *be* is:
*I/he/she/it **was***
*you/we/they **were***
   *I **was** late for work this morning.*
   *We **were** at home last night.*

To form the negative we add *-n't* or *not*. We usually only use the full form *not* in more formal contexts and for emphasis.
   *We **weren't** at home last night.*
   *No, it **was not** fun!*
   NOT *We didn't be at home last night.*
   NOT *No, it did not be fun!*

To form a question we put *was* or *were* before the subject.
   ***Were you*** at home last night?
   *What time **was the flight**?*
   *How long **was he** asleep?*
   NOT *Did you be at home last night?*

## Use

**E** We use the past simple to talk about completed past events, situations, or states.

> I **played** tennis yesterday.
> We **lived** in Scotland until I was fifteen.
> He **took** his driving test three times.
> I **was** at home all last night.
> I **didn't see** Marta last week.
> When **did** the bus leave?

We use the past simple to talk about a single event or repeated events.

> I **went out** last night.
> I **went out** three times last week.

---

### TIP

We often use the past simple with expressions of finished time such as *two hours ago, this morning, last night, yesterday, at the weekend, last week, last summer, in 2009, when I was a child*, etc.
**The bus left five minutes ago.**
**Did you go out last night?**
**I started school in 1992.**

# 15 The present perfect

## Form

A The present perfect is the present of *have* + past participle. We often use the contracted forms *'s* and *'ve*, especially in speaking.

> *I've **finished** the report.*
> *Sara**'s gone** to the supermarket.*
> *The president **has resigned**.*
> *I've **lost** my wallet.*

For a list of irregular past participles
▶ page 329.

B To form the negative we add *-n't* or *not*. We usually only use the full form *not* in more formal contexts and to give emphasis.

> *I **haven't finished**.*
> *He **hasn't phoned** yet.*
> *We **have not received** your booking.*
> *No, I **have not told** anyone!*

C To form a question we put *have/has* before the subject.

> ***Has she** left?*
> *Where **have they** gone?*
> ***Have you** finished?*
> *Why **has Jake** quit his job?*

In spoken English we sometimes contract *have* to *'ve* and *has* to *'s* after a question word.

> *Where've they gone?*
> *Why's Jake quit his job?*

## Use

D The present perfect connects the
past and present. We use it in three
basic ways.

• To talk about a past event or situation
that has an impact on the present.
> *I've lost my wallet.*
> *My bike's gone!*
> *Have you heard? Sue's resigned.*
> *At last, we've finished.*

When we use the present perfect we
do <u>not</u> say when the event occurred.
> *The plane's landed.*
> NOT *The plane's landed ten minutes ago.*

• To talk about experiences in our
lives. We use the present perfect
because the experience has some
relevance in the present.
> *Ask Harry about London. He's been
> there a few times.*
> *Do you like Mexican food? ~ I don't
> know. I've never eaten it.*

We can use *have you* (etc.) *ever ...?* to
ask about someone's life experiences.
> *Have you ever been to Scotland?*
> *Have you ever eaten Vietnamese
> food?*
> *Has Richard ever been to Australia?*

• To talk about an activity, event, or situation that started in the past and continues to the present. When we use the present perfect in this way we must use *since* or *for*.

> I*'ve had* my laptop **for** about a year.
> I **haven't seen** George **since** the conference.
> How long **have** they **been married**?
> ~ **For** about five years.

Note that we use *since* + a point in time and *for* + a period of time.

> I*'ve worked* for RBC **since August**.
> I*'ve worked* for RBC **for about six months**.
> We*'ve lived* here **since we got married**.
> We*'ve lived* here **for ten years**.

We do <u>not</u> use a present tense to talk about something that started in the past and continues to the present.

> NOT ~~We live here for six years.~~
> NOT ~~We are living here for six years.~~

---

**TIP**

To talk about a new experience, we can use *This is / It's the first* (etc.) *time* + present perfect.
**This is the third time I've stayed** in this hotel.
**Is this the first time you've been skiing?**
NOT ~~This is the third time I stay in this hotel.~~

---

41

# 16 The present perfect or past simple?

## Basic differences

A  The main differences between the present perfect and the past simple are:

- The present perfect connects the present and the past. It tells us about something in the present which is affected by something in the past. The past event either impacts on now or continues now.

    *I've lost my passport.* (My passport is lost now.)
    *Sarah's gone to the gym.* (Sarah's at the gym now.)
    *They've lived in Paris for ten years.* (They live in Paris now.)

- The past simple tells us only about the past.

    *I lost my passport on holiday.*
    *Sarah went to the gym with Julia.*
    *They lived in Paris for ten years.*

## Time expressions

B  Time expressions can refer to 'finished' time (*two minutes ago, at 3.30, yesterday, last week, in 2011*, etc.) or 'unfinished' time (*recently, this week, since 2005, so far*, etc.).

- We use the present perfect with an expression of 'unfinished' time.

*I've been* very busy **this week**.
*We've been* on holiday twice **this year**.
**Have** you **spoken** to Alex **recently**?
*I've worked* for CNN **since 2008**.

- We use the past simple with an expression of 'finished' time.
    *I was* very busy **yesterday**.
    *We went* on holiday twice **last year**.
    **Did** you **speak** to Alex **at the party**?
    *I worked* for CNN **from 2007 to 2012**.

## Finished and continuing states and actions

C We use the present perfect for something that started in the past and continues now.
    *They've lived* in Oxford for five years.
    (They live in Oxford now.)
    *We've been* friends for years.
    (We are friends now.)
    *She's played* the piano since she was a child. (She plays the piano now.)
    *He's written* several books.
    (He continues to write books.)

We use the past simple for something that finished in the past.
    *They lived* in Oxford for five years.
    (They don't live in Oxford any more.)
    *We were* friends for years. (We are not friends now.)

> *She **played** the piano when she was a child.* (She doesn't play the piano now.)
> *He **wrote** several books.* (He doesn't write books any more.)

Note that we can use *for* with both the present perfect and past simple, but we only use *since* with the present perfect.

> *I **have worked** full time **since** May.*
> *I **have worked** full time **for** months.*
> *I **worked** full time **for** months.*
> NOT *I worked full time since May.*

## News

**D** We generally use the present perfect to introduce some news and then we use the past simple for the details, such as when and how it happened. We use the present perfect to express the impact on now.

> *Ulrich's **broken** his leg. He **fell** off his ladder.*
> *Morton **has won** the UK Masters tournament. He **beat** Roger Jones.*

---

**TIP**

*It's* + time expression + *since* … is a useful structure.
> ***It's ages since** I saw a good film.*
> ***It's at least a year since** we last met.*
> ***How long is it since** you last played tennis?*

Because *since* refers to an occasion in the past, we generally use the past simple in this structure. However, it is possible to use the present perfect after *since*.
> ***It's ages since** I've seen a good film.*

# 17 The present perfect continuous

## Form

A The present perfect continuous is the present of *have* + *been* + ing-form.

*I've been waiting* for ten minutes.
*It's been raining* all day.
*I haven't been waiting* long.
How long *have* you *been working* here?

The full form is usually only used in more formal contexts and to give emphasis.

*The President has been holding meetings* all week.
*I have not been using* your computer!

## Use

B The present perfect connects the present with the past. We generally use the continuous form of the present perfect to express prolonged or repeated activity. We use it in two basic ways:

• for something that started in the past and continues now

*It's been snowing* since this morning.
*We've been eating* out a lot recently.
*I haven't been going* to the gym much this summer.

When we use the present perfect continuous in this way we often use it with a time expression (*since this morning*, *for two weeks*, *recently*, etc.).

- for something which stopped recently but which has an impact on the present

    Sorry about the mess. *I've been trying* to fix my moped.
    You're covered in oil! What *have* you *been doing*?
    It looks like it*'s been raining*.

## Present perfect continuous or simple?

C There is sometimes little difference in meaning between the present perfect continuous and the present perfect simple and in some situations both forms are possible.

How long *have* you *lived* here?
OR How long *have* you *been living* here?

D However, there are some important differences.

- We generally use the present perfect continuous to express or emphasize the length or repetition of an activity. There is a focus on the activity or the 'doing'.

    We*'ve been waiting* for over an hour.
    *Have* you *been watching* those DVDs I lent you?

*We've **been having** a lot of meetings recently.*

- We generally use the present perfect simple to express completion and result and to say 'how many times'. There is no particular focus on the 'doing'.

  *We've **had** about fifteen meetings this month.*
  *We've **waited** long enough. Let's go.*
  ***Have** you **watched** those DVDs I lent you?*
  NOT ~~We've been having about fifteen meetings this month.~~

- We tend to use the present perfect continuous for something that is seen as new, temporary, or short-term, and the present perfect simple for something that is seen as permanent or long-term.

  *She's **been living** in Stirling for about a month now.*
  *She's **lived** in Stirling for thirty years.*

---

**TIP**

We often use the present perfect continuous in conversation to talk about recent regular activities in our life.
*What **have** you **been doing** lately?*
*I've **been studying** a lot.*
*I **haven't been going** out much.*

# 18 The past continuous

## Form

**A** The past continuous is *was/were* + ing-form.

*I **was watching** TV.*
*They **were waiting** for hours.*
*We **were living** in Paris in 2010.*

**B** To form the negative we add *-n't* or *not* after *was/were*. We generally use the full form *not* for emphasis and in more formal contexts, such as in writing.

*The internet **wasn't working** this morning.*
*They **weren't trying** very hard.*
*We **were not expecting** to hear from you.*
*You **were not listening**!*

**C** To form a question we put *was/were* before the subject.

***Was** it **snowing** when you arrived?*
*What **was** Alex **wearing** last night?*
***Were** you **living** in London in 2012?*
*How long **were** you **waiting**?*

For spelling of the ing-form ▶ page 332.

## Use

**D** We use the past continuous to talk about something in progress at a specific time in the past. The activity or situation started before this time and possibly continued after it.

*We **were having** breakfast at 7.30.*
*It **wasn't raining** when I got up.*
*I didn't hear the doorbell. I **was***
***listening** to music.*

E   We also use the past continuous to
talk about an activity or situation that
continues over a period of time in
the past.
*We **were driving** all night.*
*I **was studying** for most of the day.*
*They **were waiting** for ages.*
*I **was working** on the project from May*
*to August.*

The use of the past continuous in
this way emphasizes the continuous
or repeated nature of the activity
or situation. It is often used as an
alternative to the past simple, which
expresses the activity or situation
more as a neutral fact.
*We **were driving** all night. / We **drove***
*all night.*
*They **were waiting** for ages. / They*
***waited** for ages.*
*I **was working** on the report all night. /*
*I **worked** on the report all night.*

F   We often use the past continuous with
the past simple when one action stops or
'interrupts' another. This is sometimes
called the 'interrupted past continuous'.

*We **were having** a walk by the river when it **started** raining.*
*My computer **crashed** while I **was doing** my assignment.*

We generally use *when* or *while* to link the actions.

*I was having a shower **when** you phoned.*
*My parents met **while** they were both working at the British Museum.*

G We can also use *while* when two continuous actions happen at the same time.

***While** you **were taking** it easy and watching TV, I **was cooking** dinner for everyone!*

---

**TIP**

We often use the past continuous to set the scene for events in a narrative. Notice that here *and* is also used to link the actions.

*We **were driving** along the coast road from Berwick to Alnwick and suddenly we noticed ....*
*Mrs Smithers **was doing** her daily housework when Lord Harris unexpectedly summoned her.*

---

# 19 The past perfect and past perfect continuous

## The past perfect

### Form

A The past perfect is *had* + past participle. We often use the short form *'d*, especially in speaking.

> *We'd met twice before.*
> *The film had started when we arrived.*
> *I was late, but luckily the bus hadn't left.*
> *How long had they been there before they saw her?*

For a list of irregular past participles
▶ page 329.

B With subject pronouns (*I, you, they,* etc.), the full form is usually only used in more formal contexts and to give emphasis.

> *We had expected a more detailed response.*
> *I had not finished speaking!*

### Use

C We use the past perfect to show that something happened before something else in the past or before a specific time in the past.

> *Patricia had left when we arrived.*
> *We'd finished the meeting by lunchtime.*
> *I found a magazine that someone had left behind.*

*Dinosaurs **had become** extinct by about 65 million years ago.*

D Compare the use of the past simple and the past perfect in the following sentences.

*They **started** the meeting when we arrived.* (= They started the meeting just after we arrived.)

*They'**d started** the meeting when we arrived.* (= They started the meeting before we arrived.)

## Sequence adverbs

E We often use sequence adverbs such as *when*, *after*, *until*, and *as soon as* to link the two past actions.

*I had breakfast **after I'd shaved** and **showered**.*

*I didn't buy my first car **until I'd passed** my driving test.*

*We set off **as soon as we'd had** lunch.*

## The past perfect continuous

## Form

F The past perfect continuous is *had been* + ing-form. Again, we often use the short form *'d*.

*We'**d been waiting** for about an hour.*

*It **hadn't been raining** for long.*

## Use

G Again, we are referring to something that happened before something else in the past, or before a specific time in the past. We use the past perfect continuous to show or emphasize that the activity was continuous or regularly repeated over a period of time.

> *We realized when dawn broke that we'd been working all night.*
> *I'm not surprised Dave and Jen split up. They'd been arguing for months.*

---

### TIP

We often use *already* with the past perfect to emphasize the sequence of events, and *just* to show the first action happened only a short time before the second.
*The bus **had already left** when I got there.*
*They'd just finished lunch when we arrived.*

---

# 20 *Used to* and *would*

## *Used to*

### Form

A We use *used to* + base form.

> Patrick **used to work** in Paris.
> I **used to have** a motorbike.

To form the negative we use *didn't use to* + base form.

> I **didn't use to like** football.

To form a question we put *did* before the subject.

> **Did** you **use to do** any sports at school?
> What **did** people **use to do** before mobile phones?

B Note that there is no final *-d* in negatives and questions. This is because *used to* is the past simple of the regular verb *use to* and therefore operates as other regular verbs.

> I didn't **use to** like football.
> Did you **use to** play computer games?
> NOT *I didn't used to like football.*
> NOT *Did you used to play computer games?*

## *Never* and *ever*

C For emphasis we can use *did you ever use to …?* and '*… never used to …*'.

> **Did** you **ever use to watch** 'Friends'?
> I **never used to watch** much TV.

## Use

**D** We use *used to* to talk about past situations that no longer exist. This could be:

- past habits and routines
  I **used to play** computer games all the time.
  We **used to go skiing** every year.
  Do you do any sports? ~ No, but I **used to**.

- past states
  I **used to live** in Scotland.
  There **used to be** a supermarket here.
  I **didn't use to like** coffee.

**E** *Used to* and the past simple can often have similar meaning, but *used to* gives extra emphasis that the situation no longer exists.
I **used to have** long hair when I was in my teens. / I **had** long hair when I was in my teens.

### Would

**F** We use *would* with similar meaning to *used to* to talk about past habits and routines. *Would* is usually contracted to *'d* after pronouns.
I**'d play** computer games all the time.
We**'d go skiing** every year.
My grandparents **would stay** with us every Christmas.

**G** We do not, however, use *would* to talk about past states.

> I **used to live** in Scotland.
> NOT *I would live in Scotland.*
> My dad **used to have** a beard.
> NOT *My dad would have a beard.*

**H** *Would* to talk about past habits and routines is rarely used in a negative or question form.

> We **didn't use to** get much homework at school.
> NOT *We wouldn't get much homework at school.*

## Frequency adverbs

**I** We can use frequency adverbs such as *always*, *usually*, *often*, or *sometimes* with *would* and *used to*.

> My old boss **would often arrive** late for work.
> I **sometimes used to walk** to school, but I'd **usually get** the bus.

---

### TIP

*No, but I used to*, etc. is a useful answer to a *Do you ...?* question.
*Do you play a musical instrument?* ~
**No, but I used to.**
*Does your mother work?* ~ **No, but she used to.**

# 21 Action and state verbs

A Most verbs express actions or things that happen. We can usually use them in both the simple and continuous forms.

   I **read** the paper every day.
   I**'m reading** the paper at the moment.
   Martin **works** for the BBC.
   He**'s working** in France this week.

B Some verbs express states, such as existence, feelings, or possession. We generally use them only in the simple form.

   She **looks** about forty.
   We**'ve known** each other for years.
   My mum**'s** a teacher.
   **Do** you **believe** in ghosts?
   Who **does** this bag **belong** to?
   NOT ~~She's looking about forty.~~
   NOT ~~We've been knowing each other for years.~~

C Common state verbs include verbs expressing

   • existence: *be, exist, come from*

   • thoughts and mental states: *admire, agree, believe, care, depend, expect, feel, forget, hope, imagine, know, mean, mind, realize, recognize, remember, suppose, think, understand*

- desires and likes: *prefer, need, want, enjoy, hate, like, love*

- possession: *belong, have (got), own, possess*

- appearance: *appear, look (like), seem*

- qualities: *consist of, cost, deserve, fit, involve, measure, sound, suit, weigh*

- senses: *feel, hear, see, smell, taste.*

D  We can, however, use some state verbs in the continuous form. This is when we want to emphasize that the feeling or attitude is at a particular time and temporary. The state verbs that we most commonly use like this include: *be, enjoy, expect, feel, like, love, look (like), need, think, want.*
   *I'm loving this pasta.*
   *I'm really enjoying work at the moment.*
   *We were expecting you to arrive earlier.*
   *The internet's being a bit temperamental at the moment.*

E  Some verbs can be either a state verb or an action verb according to the meaning that is expressed. These verbs include: *admire, appear, be, come, feel, fit, have, look, see, smell, sound, taste, think, weigh.*
   *That cake looks delicious.* (state verb)
   *I'm looking for my wallet.* (action verb)

*I **think** he's German.* (state verb)
*Shh! I'**m thinking**.* (action verb)
*I **weigh** 65 kg.* (state verb)
*You need **to weigh** the flour.*
(action verb)
***Does** the shirt **fit** you?* (state verb)
*My dad'**s fitting** a new tap in the
bathroom.* (action verb)

**F**  We usually use verbs of the senses
(*feel, see, hear, smell, taste*) with *can/
can't*, rather than in the present simple,
to express what we feel, see, etc. at the
time of speaking.
*I **can't hear** the TV.*
*I **can smell** gas.*
***Can** you **see** James?*
NOT *I don't hear the TV.*

The following uses are possible but are
less common.
*I **smell** gas.*
***Do** you **see** James?*

---

**TIP**

There are a number of useful
expressions with state verbs. These are
never used in the continuous form.
*It depends.  I don't mind.*
*It doesn't matter.  I don't care*
*I don't agree.  I don't know.*

---

# 22 Overview of present and past tenses

| Tense | Main uses | Examples |
|---|---|---|
| Present simple *I work* | • fact<br>• permanent situation<br>• habit, routine<br>• state of mind | *Whales **are** mammals.*<br>*They **live** in London.*<br>*I **drive** to work.*<br>*She **loves** old films.* |
| Present continuous *I am working* | • action/situation in progress now<br>• changing situation<br>• temporary situation<br>• expressing irritation | *He's **watching** TV.*<br>*The earth **is getting** hotter.*<br>*I'm **working** in Leeds this month.*<br>*He's **always taking** my laptop.* |
| Past simple *I worked* | • completed past event, situation, or state | *She **passed** her exam.*<br>*We **lived** in Paris for two years.*<br>*The film **was** great.* |
| Past continuous *I was working* | • action/situation in progress at or during a time in the past | *I **was watching** TV at 9.30.*<br>*We **were living** in the US in 2010.* |

| Present perfect *I have worked* | • past event with impact on the present<br>• life experiences<br>• something starting in the past and continuing now | I've **lost** my keys.<br>I've **been** to Turkey twice.<br>We've **lived** here since 2009.<br>He's **been** a lawyer for ten years. |
| Present perfect continuous *I have been working* | • prolonged or repeated activity that continues to now or has an impact on now | It's **been raining** for days.<br>We've **been working** since 11.30.<br>I'm **been running**. I'm exhausted. |
| Past perfect *I had worked* | • action/situation that happened before another event or time in the past | We'd **met** twice before.<br>He'd already **left** in 2008. |
| Past perfect continuous *I had been working* | • prolonged or repeated ativity up to an event or time in the past | We'd **been waiting** for over an hour when he arrived. |

There are two basic tenses: present and past. Each can also be continuous (e.g. *I was doing*) or perfect (e.g. *I have done*), or a combination (e.g. *I have been doing*).

## 23

# 23 The present subjunctive

## Form

A The present subjunctive is the same as the base form of the verb. There is no -s ending in the third person.

*They requested that she **arrive** early.*
*It is proposed that he **give** a careful account of his actions.*

With the verb *be*, we use the base form *be* with all persons.

*It is important that everyone **be** present at the meeting.*

B The negative is *not* + base form.

*They asked that we **not be** late.*
*The chairman requested that we **not start** the meeting until everyone is here.*
*He spoke to the media on condition that he **not be** identified.*

## Use

C The present subjunctive is used in very formal contexts. Its use today is quite uncommon, and can sound a little old-fashioned. It is used in two main ways.

- In a that-clause expressing a formal desire, instruction, request, suggestion, or related emotion.

  *They request that Mr Jones **report** to reception on arrival.*
  *They require that he **submit** the application by Friday.*

*I suggested that he **leave**
immediately.*
*It is our recommendation that James
Davis **not be** appointed as general
manager.*
*It is crucial that you **be** there before
Tom arrives.*
*He was released from prison on
condition that he **report** to a police
station twice every week.*

The following verbs and expressions
can be used (with or without *that*)
with the present subjunctive:
*advise, ask, command, demand, desire,
insist, propose, recommend, request,
require, suggest, urge;
it is best, it is crucial, it is desirable,
it is essential, it is imperative, it is
important, it is vital, it is a good idea,
it is a bad idea, it is recommended, it is
our recommendation, on condition.*

*We **ask** that all glasses **be** washed
before return.*
*He **commanded** we **attend** the
meeting.*
*He was allowed an extra week's leave
**on condition that** he **finish** his report
beforehand.*
***It is our recommendation that** she
**receive** a full refund.*
***It is desirable that** he **present** his
research to his students on a regular
basis.*

- In clauses beginning with *if* and *whether*.

    *If* that **be** the case, there is little more we can do.

    *Crime is on the increase, **whether** it **be** in inner cities or more rural areas.*

We can also sometimes use *should* as a more formal alternative to *if*.

  *Should that **be** the case, there is little more we can do.*

  *Please let us know, **should** you **require** any further assistance.*

---

**TIP**

It is unlikely that you will need to write or speak using the present subjunctive, but it is useful that you can recognize it. In most instances, it is more natural and common to use the present or past tense.

*The teacher insists that her students **are** on time.*

*I suggested that he **left** immediately.*

*If that's the case, there is little more we can do.*

---

# 24 The past subjunctive

## Form

A The past subjunctive is the same as the past simple form of the verb.

*It's time we **left**.*
*I'd rather you **didn't say** anything to Richard.*

Because the past subjunctive is the same as the past simple of the verb, people often use the term 'past simple' when actually referring to the past subjunctive.

The past subjunctive of *be* is *were*.
*If I **were** you, I'd be really pleased.*
*I wish I **were** ten years younger.*

## Use

B The past subjunctive is generally used to talk about imaginary or desired situations. We use it after certain words or phrases and always after a subject. The main uses of the past subjunctive are explained below.

C We use the past subjunctive after *it's time* to talk about something we need to do now or very soon.
*It's time we **went** home.*
*It's time I **started** my dissertation.*
NOT *It's time we go home.*

**D** We use the past subjunctive after
*would rather* or *would prefer* to express
desires and preferences.

> *I'd rather you **arrived** a bit before seven.*
> *I'd rather you **didn't smoke** if you
> don't mind.*
> *They'd prefer that we **met** them at
> the café.*

We also sometimes use a present tense
after *would rather* or *would prefer*.
Using the present tense makes things
sound a little more direct.

> *I'd rather you **don't smoke** if you
> don't mind.*

Note that when *would rather/prefer* is
not followed by a subject you do not
use the past subjunctive.

> *I'd rather **go** by bus.*
> NOT *I'd rather went by bus.*

**E** We use the past subjunctive after *if* and
*wish* to express something imaginary
or hypothetical or unlikely to happen.

> ***If** I **were** you, I'd look for a new job.*
> ***If** I **had** more time, I'd read a lot more.*
> *I **wish** you **were** here.*
> *I **wish** it **weren't** raining.*

For more on *if* and *wish* for imaginary
or hypothetical situations ▶ 35–37.

**F** We can use the past subjunctive after *suppose* and *imagine* when we are expressing something imaginary or hypothetical or unlikely to happen. *Suppose* and *imagine* used in this way are alternatives to *if*.

> **Suppose** you **failed** your exam. What would you do?
>
> **Imagine** you **won** the lottery. What's the first thing you'd go out and buy?

**G** Using the past subjunctive *were* can sometimes sound too formal. To sound less formal, we can generally use the past simple *was* for *I* and the third person (*he, she, it*).

> *I wish David* **were** *here.*
> OR *I wish David* **was** *here.*
> *Imagine he* **were** *here now.*
> OR *Imagine he* **was** *here now.*
> *It's time I* **were** *in bed.*
> OR *It's time I* **was** *in bed.*

---

### TIP

We use the phrase *it's high time* to emphasize that something needs to happen or change. We use *it's about time* when we are being critical.

**It's high time** politicians **stopped** making empty promises.

**It's about time** you **grew up** and **started** acting your age!

# 25 Present tenses for the future (1)

## Present simple

A We use the present simple to talk about events in the future that are part of a timetable, itinerary, or programme. We usually specify the time.

> His plane **lands** at 6.40.
> The meeting **is** on Wednesday.
> The train **leaves** soon.
> When **does** the football season **start**?
> The show **begins** at 7.30 and **finishes** at 10.30.

We often use the following verbs in the present simple to refer to the future: *be, arrive, land, take off, come, go, leave, depart, set off, start, begin, end, finish, open, close.*

## Present continuous

B We use the present continuous to talk about things in the future that are already arranged, agreed, or finalized, for example when we have made a booking or have made a firm arrangement to meet or do something with someone. We use the present continuous because we see the arrangement as existing now.

> I'**m seeing** Dan tomorrow night. We'**re going** to Café Coco.
> Sasha **isn't coming** to the meeting.

C   We can also use the present
    continuous for things which are not
    arranged with someone else, but which
    we ourselves see as finalized or certain.

    *I'm staying in tonight. I'm doing my
    homework and then I'm having an
    early night.*

D   When we use the present continuous
    to refer to the future, we often specify
    the time.

    *They're getting married **on 14th April**.
    We're going skiing **in February**.
    Are you working **tomorrow**?*

E   *Be going to* can sometimes have
    a similar meaning to the present
    continuous, and sometimes we can use
    either with little difference in meaning.

    *We're going to have pizza tonight.*
    OR *We're having pizza tonight.*

    For more detail on the similarities
    and differences between the present
    continuous and *be going to* ▶ 28.

---

**TIP**

We usually use the present continuous,
especially *are you doing*, to ask about
someone's social activities.
*Are you doing anything this evening?*
*What are you doing at the weekend?*
*Are you going out tonight?*

# 26

## 26 Present tenses for the future (2)

### Present tenses after time conjunctions

A When talking about the future, we usually use the present simple after time conjunctions such as *when*, *after*, *as soon as*, etc.

*I'll text you **when** we **get** to the hotel.*
*Call me **as soon as** Carlos **arrives**.*
*I'll be in touch again **before** I **leave**.*
*Wait here **until** I **tell** you.*
NOT ~~I'll text you when we'll get to the hotel.~~

B We can also use the present continuous after a time conjunction to express something in progress.

*I'll think of you next week **while** I'm **lying** on the beach.*
*Let me know **the next time** you're **working** here in New York.*
*I'll phone you **when** I'm **feeling** better.*
NOT ~~I'll think of you next week while I'll be lying on the beach.~~

C We can also use the present perfect to show or to emphasize that one event is completed before the other event.

*Do borrow the book **when** I've **read** it.*
*I won't decide **until** I've **seen** the reports.*
NOT ~~Do borrow the book when I'll have read it.~~

**D** The two clauses can usually go in either order. When we begin with the time conjunction we usually put a comma between the clauses.

> *I'll call you when I get to the station.*
> *When I get to the station, I'll call you.*
> *I won't know where I'm staying until I've heard from John.*
> *Until I've heard from John, I won't know where I'm staying.*

**E** Time conjunctions that are commonly used in this way include: *when, while, as soon as, after, before, until, the moment, the minute, the second, by the time, the next time*. We also use a present tense after *if*.

> *Let's wait here **until** the rain stops.*
> *I'll call you **the second** I hear any news.*
> *You must visit **the next time** you're here in Oxford.*
> *Let me know **if** you need any help with the shopping.*

## Present tenses in relative clauses

**F** When talking about the future, we use a present tense in a relative clause.

> *Anyone **who arrives late** will not be allowed to enter.*
> *Will the person **who is last to leave** please turn off the lights?*
> *We'll get **whichever bus arrives first**.*
> NOT *Anyone who will arrive late will not be allowed to enter.*

## 26

## Present tenses in noun clauses

G  When talking about the future, we use
a present tense in a noun clause that
begins with *that*, a question word, or
*if*/*whether*.

Make sure **that the windows are
closed** when you leave.
What we do will depend on **what the
weather is like**.
We have to decide **if we take the coast
road home**.
You must let me know **which train you
get**. Send me a text when you're on it.
NOT <del>Make sure that the windows will
be closed when you leave.</del>

---

### TIP

We often use a present tense after *hope*
when we are talking about the future.
I **hope** your exams **go** OK.
I **hope** it **isn't raining** when we get there.

# 27 *Be to, be about to,* etc.

## *Be to*

A  We use *be* + to-infinitive to talk about
   formal or officially arranged events. This
   is most commonly used in news reports
   and other official communications.
   *The chairman **is to hold** a press
   conference tomorrow.*
   *ID cards **are to be introduced** next year.*
   *The concert **is to take place** in Hyde
   Park on 17th July.*

B  We can use *be due/set* + to-infinitive in
   a similar way.
   *The chairman **is due to hold** a press
   conference tomorrow.*
   *ID cards **are set to be introduced**
   next year.*
   *Interviews **are due to take place** on the
   16th and 17th July.*

C  We also use *be* + to-infinitive to talk
   about a rule, order, or instruction.
   *Mum says we**'re to be** in bed by 10.30.*
   *Visitors **are to report** to the main
   reception.*

## *Be (just) about to*

D  We can use *be about* + to-infinitive for
   something happening very soon.
   *The meeting **is about to begin**.*
   *The film**'s about to start**.*

We can add *just* to say the event is happening almost immediately.
> *The film's **just about to start**.*
> *Hurry up! The shop **is just about to close**.*

We can use *be (just) about to* without the verb in short answers.
> *Have you sent that email? ~ No, but I'm **just about to**.*
> *Has the film started? ~ No, but **it's about to**.*

**E** We can use *be on the verge/point of* + ing-form with similar meaning to *be just about to*.
> *The company **is on the verge of going bankrupt**.*
> *I'm **on the point of giving up**.*

**F** We do not use time adverbs with these phrases.
> *The bus is just about to leave.*
> NOT *The bus is just about to leave in two minutes.*
> *The company is on the verge of going bankrupt.*
> NOT *The company is on the verge of going bankrupt next month.*

### Be bound/certain/sure/likely to

**G** We use *be bound/certain/sure* + to-infinitive to talk about what we think will definitely happen in the future.

*Jim's **bound to be** late – he always is!*
*The concert **is sure to be sold out**.*
*We're **certain to win** at least one gold
medal.*

We can use *be (un)likely* +
to-infinitive to express less certainty.
*The concert **is likely to be sold out**.*
*It's **unlikely to rain** for the next few
days.*

## Was to, was about to, etc.

H We can use *be (about) to* etc. in the
past tense.
*The conference **was** originally **to take
place** in Genoa, but it was moved to
Rome.*
*I **was just about to leave** when it
started raining.*
*She **was on the verge of giving up**.*

---

### TIP

News headlines generally use the to-
infinitive to express future meaning.
*BBC **to lose** 5,000 jobs*
*China **to send** human to Mars*
*Qatar **to host** World Cup*

# 28 *Be going to* for the future

## Form

**A** We use the present tense of *be* +
*going to* + base form.
> It's **going to rain**.
> I'm **going to be** late.
> We're **not going to say** anything.
> **Are** you **going to have** lunch soon?

In informal spoken English, *going to*
is generally pronounced /ˈɡʌnə/.

We generally only use the full forms
*am/is/are* and *not* in formal contexts
such as writing and for emphasis.
> Mr Holmes **is going to make** an
> announcement this afternoon.
> No, I **am not going to tell** you!

## Use

**B** We use *be going to* in two main ways.

- To talk about future plans and
intentions that were made before the
time of speaking.
> Kim's **going to set up** his own web
> page.
> Have you emailed Richard? ~ No,
> I'm **going to do** it later.
> Karl **isn't going to be** at the meeting.
> When **are** you **going to speak** to
> Steve?

The verbs most commonly used with
*be going to* when talking about plans

and intentions are: *be, have, do, get, say, take, ask, see*.

• To make predictions based on direct present evidence. In other words, there is something in the present that indicates something about the future.

*Look at the time – we're going to be late.*
*It looks like it's going to rain.*
*You crashed your dad's car! He's going to go mad.*

### *Be going to* or present continuous?

C We can sometimes use *be going to* and the present continuous in a similar way. However, we generally use *be going to* for plans and intentions and we use the present continuous for something that is arranged, agreed, or finalized.

*They're going to get married in a few years.* (plan/intention)
*They're getting married on 20th July.* (finalized arrangement)
*I'm going to take my driving test soon.* (plan/intention)
*I'm taking my driving test next week.* (finalized arrangement)

For more about the difference between *be going to* and the present continuous ▶ 30.

For the present continuous used to talk about the future ▶ 25.

D When using *be going to go*, to avoid repetition we often omit the main verb *to go*.

*We're going shopping.* (= We're going to go shopping.)
*I'm going to bed.*
*Are you going to the gym?*

### Was/were going to

E We can use *was/were going to* for plans, intentions, or predictions in the past. We can use it for things that either happened or didn't happen.

*I had a feeling the exam was going to be difficult.*
*We were going to set off after lunch, but we got a bit delayed.*

---

**TIP**

*No / Not yet, but I'm going to* is a useful response for something you intend to do, but haven't done yet.
*Have you booked the hotel yet? ~ No, but I'm going to.*
*Have you watered the plants? ~ Not yet, but I'm going to.*

---

# 29 *Will* and *shall* for the future

## *Will*

### Form

A We use *will* + base form. We generally use the contracted form *'ll*, especially in speaking.

*She**'ll be** twenty next week.*
*I**'ll see** you tomorrow.*
*James**'ll be** a little late for the meeting.*

We generally only use the full form *will* in formal contexts such as writing and for emphasis.

*I **will email** you the full details by the end of the day.*
*Stop worrying, I **will be** there at 6.30.*

B The negative of *will* is *won't* or *will not*.

*Don't worry. I **won't be** late.*
*We **won't get** home until about 9.30.*

We generally only use the full form *will not* in formal contexts and for emphasis.

*We **will not tolerate** abusive behaviour.*
*For the third time, I **will not forget** the camera!*

C For questions, we put *will* before the subject.

***Will you** be at home this evening?*
*How long **will the battery** last?*
***Will he** speak at the meeting?*

## Use

**D** When referring to the future, *will* has three basic uses.

- To express spontaneous or instant choices and decisions. This includes offers, requests, and promises.

  *I think I**'ll go** for a walk.*
  *I**'ll help** you if you like.*
  *I **won't forget**.*
  ***Will** you **help** me for a moment?*
  *My friend said she**'ll translate** it for you.*

- As a neutral way of referring to the future. This is often for something that is seen as a fact, as something inevitable, or as a matter of course.

  *Sara**'ll be** eighteen in May.*
  *I**'ll be** at work all day tomorrow.*
  *Leaders of the Eurozone countries **will meet** on Friday.*
  *Rain **will spread** north throughout the afternoon.*

- To express predictions or assumptions that are based on personal feeling or opinion.

  *I think you**'ll** really **like** the book.*
  *I think France**'ll win** 2–0.*
  *The party**'ll be** great!*

For more about *will* ▶ 79.

## *Shall*

**E** We use *shall* in two basic ways.

- We most commonly use *shall* with
  *I* and *we* in the form of a question,
  for offers and suggestions, or for
  seeking advice.
  **Shall I help** you?
  **Shall we eat out** tonight?
  *What time* **shall we** *meet*?
  *Who* **shall I contact** *about the delay*?

- Some people also sometimes use *shall*
  with *I* and *we* as an alternative to *will*.
  *I think* **I shall go** *to bed.*
  OR *I think* **I'll go** *to bed.*
  **We shan't be** *late.*
  OR **We won't be** *late.*

**F** Note that the negative of *shall* is *shan't*.
We use *shall not* in formal contexts
and for emphasis.
*We* **shall not** *tolerate acts of violence
against our staff.*

---

**TIP**

We use *shall* as the question tag for *let's*.
**Let's go** for a drink, **shall we?**
**Let's watch** a film, **shall we?**

---

## 30

# 30 *Will, be going to,* or the present continuous?

A  There is no single 'future tense' in English. We use a number of different ways of talking about the future. However, it is useful to compare and contrast some of these tenses and forms.

### *Will* or *be going to* for prediction?

B  We can use both *will* and *be going to* to make predictions. The main difference is that we generally use *will* to make predictions based on personal feeling or opinion and we use *be going to* to make predictions based on present evidence. In other words, with *be going to* there is something in the present that indicates something about the future.

> *I'm sure this rain **won't last** long. It'll be nice later.*
> *Look at that beautiful clear sky. It's going to be a lovely day.*

### *Will* or *be going to* for actions?

C  We use *will* to express spontaneous or instant choices and decisions made at the time of speaking. We use *be going to* to talk about something planned or intended before the moment of speaking.

> *You need a haircut. ~ Really? OK, I'll **make** an appointment.*

*You need a haircut.* ~ *I know. I'm going to get it cut this afternoon actually.*

### *Be going to* or the present continuous for plans, intentions, and arrangements?

D The main difference between *be going to* and the present continuous is that we generally use *be going to* for plans and intentions and we use the present continuous for something that is arranged, agreed, or finalized – in other words, we use the present continuous for something that is more than just a plan or intention.

> *They're going to get married* in a couple of years. (plan/intention)
> *They're getting married* on 20th July. (finalized arrangement)

E However, sometimes it isn't clear whether a situation is a plan/intention or an arrangement. In this case there is little difference in meaning between *be going to* and the present continuous.

> *I'm going to do* my homework tonight. OR *I'm doing* my homework tonight.

F Even if something is arranged or finalized, we tend to use *be going to* when we actually travel to a place to do something. This is particularly common with the verb *see*.

*I'm going to see* a band on Saturday.
*We're going to see* the new James Bond
film tonight.

## *Will, be going to,* or the present continuous for events?

G As mentioned, we generally use *be going to* to talk about future plans and intentions and the present continuous to talk about future arrangements. However, we often use *will* as a neutral way to talk about future plans and arrangements. This is because we want to avoid suggesting anything about intention and we see the future event or situation as a fact that is inevitable or a matter of course.

*I'll be* at work all day tomorrow.
*Will* you *be* at the Madrid conference?

H News stories often use *will* as a way to express things factually and with impartiality.

*Leaders of the Eurozone countries will meet on Friday.*

---

### TIP

We often use either *be going to* or the present continuous when we first mention something, and then we use *will* after that.
Jim *'s going to read* the report on Friday.
He *will give* his comments next week.
I *'m catching* the train home tonight. I *'ll get* the 7 o'clock.

---

# 31 The future continuous, future perfect, and future perfect continuous

## Future continuous

### Form

A  We use *will be* + ing-form.
   *We'll be having* lunch at one-thirty.
   *We won't be using* DVDs in a few years' time.
   *Will you be staying* long?

### Use

B  We use the future continuous for something in progress at a specific time or over a period of time in the future.
   *I'll be driving* to work at 7.30.
   This time tomorrow, *I'll be lying* on the beach.
   *We'll be travelling* all day.
   *I'll be doing* exams for most of July.
   *I'll phone you around seven. ~ We'll be having* dinner then. Can you phone nearer to six?

C  We also use the future continuous as an alternative to *be going to* or the present continuous when we want to avoid suggesting anything about intention or arrangement. We use the future continuous in this way to express events as inevitable facts or as a matter of course.

*I'm sure I'll be seeing Harry soon.*
*We'll be spending New Year at my parents' as usual.*
*The bus **will be stopping** at Terminals 1, 3, and 5.*
***Will** Lara **be coming** with you?*
*How long **will** you **be staying** in Washington?*

## Future perfect

### Form

D We use *will have* + past participle.
*I'll **have been** here for ten years in July.*
*We'll **have finished** the meeting by midday.*
*They **won't have left** before lunch.*
*We're meeting at 7.30. **Will** you **have eaten**?*

### Use

E We use the future perfect to look back at something from a point in the future. This event may be completed or still in progress.
*We'll **have left** by midnight.*
*Sue **will have worked** here for ten years in January.*
*I'll **have gone to bed** by the time you get back.*
***Will** you **have finished** the report by Friday?*

## Future perfect continuous

F We can use the continuous form of the future perfect to focus on continuing activity, but this is not common. The form is *will have been* + ing-form.

*Next week, I'll **have been working** here for two years.*

### Be going to

G We can use *be going to* instead of *will* in these continuous and perfect structures to express an intention/plan or for a prediction based on present evidence.

*I guess I'm going to be working late tonight.*

*I'm not going to have finished this by the end of the day.*

*Suzy's going to be staying in Prague for a few weeks later in the year.*

---

**TIP**

We often use the future continuous and future perfect with *by* and *by the time*.
**By the end of the 21st century**, humans will be living on the moon.
I'll have finished the report **by the end of the day**.
I'll have got married **by the time I'm 30**.

---

# 32 Overview of future tenses

| Tense | Main uses | Examples |
|---|---|---|
| Present simple *I work* | • timetabled event or part of itinerary or programme | *The bus leaves at 4.20.* *The film starts at 6.45.* |
| Be (about) to, etc. *I am to work* *I am just about to work* | • be to: formal or officially arranged event • be (just) about to: event happening very soon | *The prime minister is to give a statement this afternoon.* *The film is about to start* *We're just about to have lunch.* |
| Present continuous *I am working* | • arranged, agreed, or finalized event | *We're meeting at 7.30.* *They're getting married in June.* |
| Be going to *I am going to work* | • plan or intention • prediction based on present evidence | *They're going to get married.* *It looks like it's going to rain.* *We're going to get wet.* |

| | | |
|---|---|---|
| Will<br>*I will work* | • spontaneous decision<br>• future inevitability or fact<br>• personal prediction or assumption | *I'll answer the phone.*<br>*She'll be twenty-one next month.*<br>*You'll love the film.*<br>*I think Spain will win.* |
| Shall<br>**Shall** *I work?* | • (only with *I* and *we*) offer,<br>suggestion, or request for advice | **Shall** *I make dinner?*<br>*Where shall we meet?* |
| Future continuous<br>*I will be working* | • event in progress at a time in the<br>future<br>• event that is a matter of course or<br>future fact | *I'll be driving to work at 7.30.*<br>*We'll be working all day.*<br>*I'll be seeing Jack soon.*<br>*Sam will be joining us later.* |
| Future perfect<br>*I will have worked* | • situation (either finished or<br>continuing) regarded from a point<br>in the future | *I'll have had lunch by 1.30.*<br>*Next month, I'll have worked<br>here for ten years.* |
| Future perfect<br>continuous<br>*I will have been working* | • continuing situation regarded from<br>a point in the future | *On 25 May, we'll have been<br>living here for exactly ten years.* |

# 33 Introduction to conditionals

A Most conditionals have two clauses: the if-clause and the main clause.

If-clause:
*If we miss the bus*, we'll get a taxi.
*If I could afford it*, I'd buy a new computer.
*If you're going to be late*, phone me.

Main clause:
If we miss the bus, **we'll get a taxi**.
If I could afford it, **I'd buy a new computer**.
If you're going to be late, **phone me**.

B The if-clause and main clause can go in either order. When the if-clause comes at the beginning, it is followed by a comma. When it is at the end, there is no comma.

If you're hungry, you'd better get something to eat.
You'd better get something to eat if you're hungry.
If it wasn't raining, we could go for a walk.
We could go for a walk if it wasn't raining.
If you'd taken a map, you wouldn't have got so lost.
You wouldn't have got so lost if you'd taken a map.

**C** We can use many different verb forms and tenses in conditional sentences.

- For conditionals that express situations that are real or possible ('real conditionals'), we usually use a present tense in the if-clause and a present tense or modal verb in the main clause.

    *If the ink **is** low, the red light **flashes**.*
    *If we **miss** the bus, we'**ll get** a taxi.*
    *If you'**re feeling** tired, **go** to bed.*
    *If you'**ve finished** your work, you **can leave**.*
    *If you'**re going to be** late, **could** you **phone** me?*

- For conditionals that express unreal or hypothetical situations ('unreal conditionals'), we use a past tense in the if-clause and *would* or a modal verb in the main clause. We use the past tense and *would* to show that we are referring to something hypothetical.

    *If I **could** afford it, I'**d buy** a new mobile.*
    *If it **wasn't raining**, we **could have** a game of tennis.*
    *If I'**d known** about the meeting, I **would have gone** to it.*
    *You **wouldn't be** so tired if you'**d gone** to bed earlier last night.*

**33**

**D** There are some verb forms and tenses that often go together in conditional sentences. These conditionals are looked at more closely in the units that follow.

Type 0: *If the ink **is** low, the orange light **comes** on.* ▶ 34.

Type 1: *If it **rains**, we'll **get** wet.* ▶ 34.

Type 2: *If I **had** more time, I'd **read** a lot more.* ▶ 35.

Type 3: *If we'd **left** earlier, we **wouldn't have missed** the bus.* ▶ 36.

Imperative conditional: *If you're tired, **go** to bed.* ▶ 34.

---

### TIP

We can use many different combinations of tenses and verb forms in conditional sentences as well as those above. Try to note the different combinations as you see and hear them.

*If you're **feeling** tired, you **should go** to bed.*

*If you're **going to be** late, **let** me know.*

*When I was at school, if we **didn't do** our homework, we **got** a detention.*

*If I **didn't like** the shirt, I **wouldn't have bought** it.*

## 34 Type 0, Type 1, and imperative conditionals

**A** Type 0, Type 1, and imperative conditionals express something real or possible.

### Type 0

**B** A Type 0 conditional is *if* + present tense + present tense. We use it for facts and situations that are always true, or when one thing automatically follows another.

> *If the ink **is** low, the orange light **comes** on.*
> *If you **freeze** water, it **expands**.*
> *If the company **goes** bankrupt, **do** we **get** our money back?*

### Type 1

**C** A Type 1 conditional is *if* + present tense + *will/'ll*. We use it for possible future situations.

> *If we **miss** the bus, we'**ll get** a taxi.*
> *If there's fish on the menu, I'**ll have** that.*
> *If it **rains** this afternoon, we **won't go out**.*
> *If you **have** time later, **will** you **email** me the photos?*

We do not normally use *will* in the if-clause.

> NOT ~~If we'll miss the bus, we'll get a taxi.~~

## 34

**D** As well as *will*, we can also use other modal verbs (*can*, *might*, etc.) and *be going to*.

*If you're not busy, **can** you **help** me?*
*If we leave now, we **might get** there in time.*
*If we don't hurry up, we**'re going to miss** the train.*

### Imperative conditional

**E** An imperative conditional is *if +* present tense + imperative. We can use it for instructions, suggestions, and advice.

*If you're tired, **go** to bed.*
*If you're cold, **put** the heating on.*
*If you **don't like** it, **don't eat** it.*

### Other tenses in the if-clause

**F** In Type 0, 1, and imperative conditionals we can also use the present continuous, the present perfect, and *be going to* in the if-clause.

*If the internet **isn't working**, turn the modem on and off.*
*If you**'ve finished** your work, you can leave.*
*Will you call me, if you**'re going to be** late?*

## Type 0 and 1 conditionals for the past

G  We can use Type 0 and 1 conditionals
   to express situations in the past. We
   change the tenses to the past tense.
   *If we **were** ever late for class, our
   teacher **got** really angry.*
   *If we **didn't have** lectures the next day,
   we **would** usually **stay up** late talking
   or watching TV.*

## *Should I/ it/ we ...*

H  We can use *should I/it/we ...* , etc. +
   present subjunctive as a more formal
   alternative to *if* + present tense ▶ 23.
   ***Should** we **be** late, start without us.*
   OR *If we're late, start without us.*
   ***Should** it **rain**, we'll move inside the
   marquee.*
   OR *If it **rains**, we'll move inside the
   marquee.*

   We can also use *if* + *should* together
   in the same clause. This is even more
   formal.
   *If it **should rain**, we'll move inside the
   marquee.*

---

### TIP

We can use *will* in an if-clause to make
polite and formal requests.
*If you**'ll take** a seat, Mr Jones will be
with you in a minute.*
*If you**'ll just wait** a moment, I'll see
what I can do.*

---

# 35

## 35 Type 2 conditional

A  A Type 2 conditional is *if* + past tense + *would(n't)*. We use a Type 2 conditional to express something imaginary or hypothetical about the present or future.

> If I **had** more time, I'**d read** a lot more.
> I'**d get** a new computer if I **could afford** it.

Note that *would* is usually contracted to *'d*, especially in speaking and informal writing.

B  There is no conditional tense in English. In the if-clause we use the past tense to express something imaginary or hypothetical.

> If I **had** a bigger garden, I'd plant some vegetables.
> I'd get some cash if I **could find** an ATM.

We do not normally use *would* in the if-clause.

> NOT ~~If I would have a bigger garden~~ ~~....~~

In the main clause we use *would(n't)* to express something imaginary or hypothetical.

> If I had a bigger garden, I'**d plant** some vegetables.
> I'**d get** some cash if I could find an ATM.

**C** We can also use the past continuous in the if-clause to express something in progress.

*If it **wasn't raining**, I'd go for a walk.*
*I'd call her if my phone **was working**.*

**D** We can also use other modals verbs such as *could* and *might* in the main clause.

*If it wasn't raining, we **could play** tennis.*
*If I had more money, I **might get** a new laptop.*

**E** In the if-clause, with *I/he/she/it* we can use *was* or *were*. Some people say that the use of *were* is more correct, but it is usually down to speaker choice.

*If I **was** younger, I'd take up skiing.*
OR *If I **were** younger, I'd take up skiing.*

*Were* used in this way is an example of the past subjunctive ▶ 24.

**F** We can use *were … to …* as a more formal alternative to *if* + past tense.

***Were** the president **to resign**, the vice-president would initially take charge.*
OR ***If** the president **resigned**, the vice-president would initially take charge.*

---

**TIP**

*If I were you, I'd …* is a useful phrase to give advice.
***If I were you, I'd** stop smoking.*
***I'd** get a haircut **if I were you**.*

# 36 Type 3 conditional

A A Type 3 conditional is *if* + past
perfect + *would(n't) have* + past
participle. We use a Type 3 conditional
to express something imaginary or
hypothetical about the past.

*If I'd **known** about the concert, I'd
**have gone**.* (I didn't know about the
concert, so I didn't go.)
*You **wouldn't have lost** the files if
you'd **backed** them **up**.*
(You lost the files because you didn't
back them up.)
*If we'd **taken** the satnav, we **wouldn't
have got** lost.*
*I'd **have got** some cash if I'd **been able**
to find an ATM.*

Note that *had* and *would* are both
usually contracted to *'d*, especially in
speaking and informal writing.

B In the if-clause we use the past perfect
to express something imaginary or
hypothetical in the past.

*If you'd **left** earlier, you'd have arrived
on time.*
*I would have bought your bike if I'd
**known** you were selling it.*

We do not normally use *would* in the
if-clause.

NOT *If you would have left earlier….*

**C** In the main clause we use *would(n't) have* + past participle to express something imaginary or hypothetical in the past.

> *If you'd left earlier, you'd have arrived on time.*
> *I would have bought your bike if I'd known you were selling it.*

In speaking, we often contract both *would* and *have*.

> *If I'd had more time, I'd've stayed a bit longer.*
> *I'd've spoken to her if she hadn't looked so unfriendly.*

**D** We can also use the past perfect continuous in the if-clause to express something that was in progress.

> *If it hadn't been raining, we could've gone for a walk.*
> *I'd have emailed you if the internet had been working.*

**E** We can also use other modal verbs such as *could* and *might* in the main clause.

> *If it hadn't been raining, we could've gone for a walk.*
> *If we'd thought about it a bit more, we might've been a bit more successful.*

**F** In informal speaking, you may hear people saying *if I'd have/'ve ...* in the if-clause. While some people consider this to be acceptable, especially in some local regions, many people regard it as incorrect.

*If I'd've seen you, I'd have stopped to say 'hello'.*

OR *If I'd seen you, I'd have stopped to say 'hello'.*

G We can use *had I/we* … , etc. as a more formal alternative to *if* + past perfect.

**Had** we **known** about the danger, we could have acted sooner.

OR *If we had known about the danger, we could have acted sooner.*

H We can mix Type 2 and Type 3 conditionals. This is when we are connecting the past and the present.

*If I didn't like the band, I wouldn't have gone to see them, would I?*

*If you'd gone to bed a bit earlier, you wouldn't be so tired now.*

---

**TIP**

We can use *if only* to add emphasis to a Type 3 conditional.

**If only** it hadn't been raining, we could've gone for a walk.

**If only** you'd told me earlier, I wouldn't have said anything.

---

# 37 *Wish* and *if only*

## *Wish*

**A** We use *wish* + clause to say that we want things to be different from how they are.

> I **wish I could play the piano**.
> I **wish I had more time**.
> Look at the traffic! I **wish we'd left a bit earlier**.
> I **wish it would stop raining**.

**B** After *wish* we use a past verb form in the clause to show we are expressing something imaginary or hypothetical. This is similar to the use of past tenses in some conditional sentences ▶ 33–36.

- To talk about the present, we use *wish* + past tense.
  > I **wish I had** more money.
  > I **wish it didn't rain** so much here.
  > I **wish it wasn't raining**.

- To talk about future arrangements and plans, we use *wish* + past continuous.
  > I **wish I wasn't going out** tonight.
  > I **wish you were coming** on holiday with us.

- To talk about the past, we use *wish* + past perfect.
  > I **wish I hadn't eaten** so much –
  > I feel sick.
  > I **wish I'd taken** your advice.

**37**

**C** To express that we want something to change in the future, we use *wish* + clause with *would*.

> *I wish my kids would phone me a bit more often.*
> *I wish it would stop raining.*
> *We all wish the government would do something about unemployment.*

We often use *wish* + *would* to express annoyance or irritation.

> *I wish you'd listen for once!*
> *I wish you wouldn't do that!*

In a clause with *would*, the subject in the clause cannot be the same as the subject of the main verb *wish*.

> NOT *I wish I would work less.*

**D** Note that the clause following *wish* can sometimes begin with *that*.

> *I wish that I had more money.*
> OR *I wish I had more money.*

The clause must have a subject (*I, you, David, my computer*, etc.).

> *I wish I could play the piano.*
> NOT *I wish could play the piano.*

## If only

**E** *If only* has similar meaning to *wish*, but it is generally more emphatic.

> *If only I had more money.*
> *Look at the traffic! If only we'd left a bit earlier.*
> *If only you'd listen for once!*

We can add a second clause after
*if only* ▶ 36 TIP.
   **If only** *I'd been listening, I'd know
   what to do.*

### Wish to

F   We can use *wish* + to-infinitive as a
   formal alternative to *want/would like* +
   to-infinitive.
      *I **wish to speak** to the manager.*
      *Please inform us if you **wish to take**
      the matter further.*

G   We do not use *wish* + noun.
      *I **wish to make** an appointment with
      the manager.*
      NOT ~~I wish an appointment with the
      manager.~~

---

**TIP**

We use *wish* in a number of phrases to
express our good wishes for someone.
*I **wish** him **well**.*
*We **wish** you **every success** in the future.*
*We **wish** you **a happy birthday**.*

---

# 38 Introduction to the passive

For forms of the passive ► 39.

A We use the passive to say what happens to something or someone. We use the active to say what someone or something does. Compare these passive and active sentences.

Passive:
*The Mini **is made** in Oxford.*
*Chelsea **were beaten** by Barcelona.*

Active:
*They **make** the Mini in Oxford.*
*Barcelona **beat** Chelsea.*

B Note that the subject of a passive sentence (the Mini, Chelsea, etc.) is the object of the active sentence. For passive sentences with two objects ► 2.

C The most common reason for using the passive is when we do not say who or what does the action. This is usually because the person or thing that does the action (called 'the agent') is obvious, unknown, not important, or we do not want to say who it is.
*Billions of SMS messages **are sent** every day.*
*My bike **was stolen** last week.*

*The World Cup **is held** every four years.*
*Two people **were killed** in the accident.*
*I admit that mistakes **have been made**.*

## Passive with *by*

D Sometimes we do want to say who or
what the agent is, usually when this is
providing new information about an
existing topic. We use *by* to introduce
the agent.

*Was it Spielberg who directed 'Avatar'? ~*
*No, it **was directed by** James Cameron.*
*The house **was designed by** Edwin Lutyens.*

## *You, we, they, people* + active

E In informal contexts, especially in
speaking, we often avoid using the
passive by using the active with the
subjects *you*, *we*, *they*, or *people*. This
often occurs when referring to 'people
in general'. Compare the following:

*You, we*, etc. + active verb:
*  **Can you buy** tickets in advance?*
*  **We should do more** to protect the
  environment.*
*  **People don't play** board games much
  these days.*

Passive verb:
*  **Can** tickets **be bought** in advance?*
*  More **should be done** to protect the
  environment.*
*  Board games **aren't played** much
  these days.*

We can also use *someone* to refer to a specific, but unknown, person.
**Someone has taken** my coat.

## Verbs without a passive form

F Intransitive verbs (verbs which do not take an object) do not have a passive form.

*We arrived at the station.*
NOT ~~The station was arrived at.~~

G Some state verbs that take an object do not have a passive form. The most common of these include: *have* (possession), *mind*, *look like*, *cost*, *fit*, *suit*, *lack*.

*People have 206 bones in their body.*
NOT ~~206 bones are had by people in their body.~~

Most state verbs that take an object do have a passive form.

*He **is known** all over the world.*
*The castle **is owned** by Lord Jenkins.*

---

**TIP**

One common use of the passive is in more formal contexts, when we want to use an impersonal style, such as in factual writing and for rules and procedures.
*The research **was carried out** in twenty countries.*
*Unattended bags **will be removed** and possibly **destroyed**.*

---

# 39 Passive forms

For uses of the passive ▶ 38.

A To form the passive we use *be* + past participle.
> *The rooms **are cleaned** every day.*
> *The modern bicycle **was invented** in the 1830s.*
> *The animals **have been fed**.*

B For the negative, we use *-n't* or *not* after the auxiliary verb.
> *The rooms **aren't cleaned** every day.*
> *The euro **isn't used** in the UK.*
> *I **wasn't told** about the meeting.*

We can use the full negative form *is not*, *were not*, etc. in formal situations and for emphasis.
> *Smoking **is not permitted** in the building.*
> *I **was not informed** of the changes.*

C In a question, we put the subject after the auxiliary.
> ***Is the competition held** every year?*
> *Where **was this photo taken**?*

D For passive forms with two or more auxiliary verbs, *-n't/not* goes after the first auxiliary in a negative, and the subject goes after the first auxiliary in a question.

*A final decision hasn't been made yet.*
*Has the room been cleaned yet?*
*Have the animals been fed?*

E  We can use different tenses in the passive:

- present and past simple
  *The championships are held every two years.*
  *How often is the website updated?*
  *The museum was opened by the Queen.*

- present and past continuous
  *The office is being decorated at the moment.*
  *The room was being cleaned when I arrived.*

- present and past perfect
  *The meeting has been cancelled.*
  *Have Alex and Suzy been invited to the party?*
  *The room hadn't been cleaned when we arrived.*

## Modal verbs in the passive

F  We use the passive infinitive (*be done, be made, be opened*, etc.) after a modal verb and after *have to* and *need to*.
  *The museum will be opened by the Queen.*
  *Some music and films can be downloaded for free.*

*All rooms **must be vacated** by midday.*
*The plants **need to be watered** daily.*

G We also use the passive infinitive after
*be going to.*
*The album **is going to be released***
*in April.*

H We also use the passive infinitive after
*be to.*
*Elections **are to be held** early next year.*

I After modal verbs, *was/were going to*,
and *was/were to* we can also use a past
passive infinitive (*have been done, have
been made*, etc.).
*The flight **might have been delayed**.*
*Let's check.*
*The photocopier **should have been
fixed** yesterday, but the engineer
didn't arrive.*
*The school **was to have been opened**
by the mayor, but he was ill.*

---

### TIP

*Was/Were born* is a common use of
the passive.
*I **was born** in 1997.*
*Where **were** you **born**?*

It is actually the passive form of the
verb *bear* (past *bore*, as in *The queen
**bore** five children during her reign.*).
The active use of *bear* in this sense is
now very formal or old-fashioned.

## 40

# 40 The passive with *get* and *have*

## Passive with *get*

**A** We can sometimes use the passive with *get* rather than with *be*. We generally use *get* in informal contexts, especially in spoken English.

**B** We use *get* most commonly for things that are unplanned or unexpected.
> *The park **got vandalized**.*
> *Sorry I'm late. I **got stopped** by the police.*

**C** We do not use *get* for planned actions.
> *Construction of the new railway **was started** in 2012.*
> NOT ~~Construction of the new railway got started in 2012.~~

But we can sometimes use *get* for something that is part of a routine.
> *The bins **get emptied** once a week.*

**D** For negatives and questions we use the auxiliary verb *do*.
> *Why **did** you **get stopped** by the police?*
> *How often **do** the windows **get cleaned**?*

## *Have/get something done*

**E** The form is *have/get* + object + past participle.
> *We **have the car serviced** every year.*
> *Eric **had his flat valued** last week.*
> *I'm **getting my hair cut** tomorrow.*

**F** We use *have/get something done* as
an alternative passive structure to say
that someone does something for us,
usually when we have arranged it. We
generally use *get* in more informal
contexts, especially in speaking.

> *We're **having** our photo **taken** at
> school tomorrow.*
> *I'm going to **get** a key **cut**.*

We sometimes call this structure
'causative *have/get*' because the
subject *causes* something to happen.

We can also use *get something done*
for things that we do ourselves. We do
not normally use *have* in this way.

> *I need to **get** my assignment **finished**.*

### Have something happen

**G** We also use *have something happen*
to say that something unwelcome or
unpleasant happens to you. We do not
normally use *get* in this way.

> *I've **had** my wallet **stolen**.*
> *Paul's **had** his apartment **broken into**.*

---

**TIP**

We often use *have/get something
done* to talk about cosmetic or medical
procedures.
*I need to **get** my hair **cut**.*
*You ought to **get** your eyes **tested**.*
*Daria's **had** her ears **pierced**.*

# 41 Passive reporting structures

**A** We can use passive reporting structures to report general opinion. These structures are generally used in more formal situations such as in news reports and scientific and academic contexts.

*It is thought that the president will announce his resignation later today.*
*It has been suggested that diet is a major factor in causing the disease.*
*The hot weather is expected to continue for several more days.*

## Form

**B** There are two main passive reporting structures:

- *it* + passive verb + *that*
  *It is expected that the court case will last four weeks.*
  *It is said that breaking a mirror brings you bad luck.*
  *It has been reported that over 100 people were injured in the accident.*
  *It was once thought that the sun went round the earth.*

- subject + passive verb + to-infinitive
  *The court case is expected to last four weeks.*
  *The newly discovered planet is thought to resemble earth in many ways.*

112

*Cameron's latest film is said to be* his most epic to date.
*There are believed to be* over a septillion stars in the universe.

C Note that you can also use perfect and continuous forms of the infinitive.
*A lion is reported to have escaped* from Whitecross Zoo.
*TV presenter Sam Smith is rumoured to be dating* actress Jenny Jones.

D Verbs that are commonly used in passive report structures include: *accept, allege, assume, believe, claim, consider, expect, fear, feel, find, hope, know, prove, recommend, report, rumour, say, show, state, suggest, suppose, think, understand.*

*Hope, suggest,* and *recommend* are only normally used in the structure *it + passive verb + that.*
*It is hoped that* the parties will reach agreement by the end of the day.
NOT ~~The parties are hoped to reach agreement by the end of the day.~~

*Suppose* is only used in the structure subject + passive verb + to-infinitive.
*Women are supposed to be* better drivers than men.
NOT ~~It is supposed that women are better drivers than men.~~

## Passive verb + to-infinitive

**E** We can use a passive verb + to-infinitive when we are reporting orders, requests, and permission, etc. We generally use this structure in more formal contexts.

*I **was asked to wait** here.*
*Air travellers **have been told to expect** long delays.*
*All visitors **are requested to report** to reception on arrival.*
*I **was** always **encouraged to be** myself.*

Verbs that we commonly use in this way include: *advise, allow, ask, authorize, challenge, compel, encourage, entitle, expect, force, instruct, invite, make, mean, oblige, order, permit, persuade, remind, request, require, tell, urge, warn.*

---

### TIP

*Allow* and *let* can have similar meaning and use:
*My boss **allowed** me **to leave** work early today.*
OR *My boss **let** me **leave** work early today.*
However, we do not use *let* in the passive.
*I **was allowed to leave** work early today.*
NOT ~~I was let to leave work early today.~~

---

# 42 The passive to-infinitive and gerund

## Passive to-infinitive

A  The passive to-infinitive is *to be* + past participle (*to be decided, to be chosen*, etc.). The perfect passive to-infinitive, which refers to the past, is *to have been* + past participle (*to have been decided, to have been chosen*, etc.).

B  Some structures require the use of the to-infinitive (*We've arranged **to meet**; I was the last **to leave**;* etc.). When there is passive meaning, we use the passive to-infinitive.

> *We've arranged **to be met** at the airport.*
> *I'm always the last **to be told**!*
> *I was surprised **to be chosen** for the team.*
> *The problem seems **to have been caused** by a virus.*

## Passive gerund

C  The passive gerund is *being* + past participle (*being seen, being found*, etc.). The perfect passive gerund, which refers to the past, is *having been* + past participle (*having been seen, having been found*, etc.).

D  Some structures require the use of a gerund (*I'm fed up with **waiting**; They left without **saying** goodbye;* etc.).

When there is passive meaning, we use the passive gerund.

*I'm fed up with **being treated** like this.*
*They escaped without **being seen**.*
*The protestors risk **being arrested**.*
*There's no sign of anything **having been stolen**.*

### Need/want + gerund

E The gerund has passive meaning after *need* (*It needs painting.* = *It needs to be painted.*).

*The grass **needs cutting**.*
*My computer **needs looking at**.*
*What time **does** Jim **need picking up** from the station?*

We also use *want* in this way, as an informal, and mainly spoken, alternative to *need*.

*This milk **wants drinking** before it goes off.*

### To-infinitive or passive to-infinitive?

F In some structures, when there is passive meaning we can sometimes use either a to-infinitive or a passive to-infinitive. These include:

• after the subject *there*
  *There's a lot of work **to do**.*
  OR *There's a lot of work **to be done**.*
  *Is there much **to see**?*
  OR *Is there much **to be seen**?*

If we express the same thing using subject + *have/have got*, we cannot use the passive to-infinitive.

> *We've got a lot of work **to do***.
> NOT *We've got a lot of work to be done.*

• after an adjective

> *Is your assignment ready **to submit**?*
> OR *Is your assignment ready **to be submitted**?*
> *It's too expensive **to build**.*
> OR *It's too expensive **to be built**.*
> *My kids aren't old enough **to leave** alone.*
> OR *My kids aren't old enough **to be left** alone.*

---

**TIP**

You often see the passive to-infinitive used in news headlines that refer to the future.
*Ten hospitals **to be closed**.*
*Troops **to be withdrawn**.*
*Elections **to be held** in March.*

## 43 Overview of passive tenses and forms

| Tense/form | Passive | Example of passive |
|---|---|---|
| Present simple | am/is/are done | *The competition is held every year.* |
| Present continuous | am/is/are being done | *Our office is being decorated at the moment.* |
| Past simple | was/were done | *Google was launched in 1998.* |
| Past continuous | was/were being done | *The house was being renovated last summer.* |
| Present perfect | have/has been done | *The meeting has been cancelled.* |
| Past perfect | had been done | *By 2000, a billion web pages had been set up.* |
| be to | am/is/are to be done | *Elections are to be held in April.* |
| be going to | am/is/are going to be done | *My job title is going to be changed.* |

| | | |
|---|---|---|
| will | will be done | The new law **will be introduced** next year. |
| modal verbs | can be done | We **can be contacted** until 5.30. |
| | might be done | I think David **might be invited** to the party. |
| past modal verbs | could have been done | You **could have been hurt**. |
| | might have been done | I think Jack **might have been promoted**. |
| to-infinitive | to be done | The car needs **to be taxed** this month. |
| perfect to-infinitive | to have been done | We seem **to have been removed** from the list. |
| gerund | being done | Several games are in danger of **being called off**. |
| perfect gerund | having been done | He has no memory of **having been involved** in an accident. |

44

# 44 Reporting (*say* and *tell*)

A We can use *say* and *tell* to report what someone says (or what they write). Sometimes we report the exact or very similar words and sometimes we report the general meaning with a summary of what was said.

> He **said** he was going home.
> I **told** Alex you won't be there.
> She **says** she doesn't like Chinese food.
> Pete **tells** me it's your birthday next week.

For other reporting verbs (*promise*, *invite*, *suggest*, etc.) ▶ 46.

B We use an indirect object after *tell* and we do not use an indirect object after *say*. In other words, when we mention the hearer, we use *tell* and when we do not mention the hearer, we use *say*.

> He **said** he'd be late.
> He **told** Karen he'd be late.
> Dr Wickham **said** it was in room 213.
> Dr Wickham **told us** it was in room 213.
> NOT ~~He said Karen he'd be late.~~
> NOT ~~He told he'd be late.~~

## Say that, tell someone that

C We can use *that* when reporting. There is no rule about the use of *that* and it is often personal choice.

> She **said** she was tired.

OR *She **said that** she was tired.*
*He **told me** he was OK.*
OR *He **told me that** he was OK.*
*Sam **says** he's looking for a new job.*
OR *Sam **says that** he's looking for a new job.*

## Say/tell + question word

D We can use *say/tell* + question word (*what, why*, etc.) when we are not reporting precise information.
*Jenny **told me what** happened.*
*She **didn't say who** phoned.*
***Did** John **say why** he left so early?*
***Has** Nina **told you where** we're meeting?*

Note that we do not usually use *say* + question word in a positive statement.
NOT *Jenny said what happened.*

## Say + to

E We can sometimes use *say* + *to*. This is usually when we are not specifying what was said.
*She **said** something **to us** about the meeting.*
***Did** you **say** anything **to Harry**?*
*What **did** he **say to you**?*

We also use *say* + *to* when we are reporting instuctions or arrangements.
*Karen **said to** meet her at 6.30 outside the cinema.*

## Tense change

F When reporting, we sometimes change
the tense (present tense → past tense,
will → would, etc.) ▶ 47.

> 'I'm tired.' → She said she **was** tired.
> 'I'll text you.' → He told me he'**d** text me.
> 'I **don't** like spicy food.' → He said he
> **didn't** like spicy food.

## The imperative

G We use a to-infinitive to report an
imperative or an instruction. We
usually use *tell*, not *say*.

> 'Don't be late.' → He **told us not to
> be** late.
> 'Please be more careful.' → She **told me
> to be** more careful.

---

**TIP**

We can use *think* and *reckon*, usually
in the present tense, when we report
someone's opinion, understanding, etc.
Sam **thinks** they'll be here by about 6.30.
Erica **reckons** the meeting is on
Wednesday.
I **reckon** it's a bad idea.

# 45 Reporting questions (*ask, want to know, wonder*)

**A** We can report questions using verbs such as *ask*, *want to know*, and *wonder*.
> She **asked** me how old I was.
> Ben **wants to know** when we're going.
> He **wondered** if we wanted to go out tonight.

**B** When we want to mention the hearer we use *ask* + indirect object. We do not use *want to know* and *wonder* with an indirect object.
> He **asked me** where I lived.
> NOT *He wondered me where I lived.*

However, we can also use *ask* without mentioning the hearer.
> I **asked** how much it costs.
> **Did** you **ask** how often he sees her?

**C** We can use *ask*, *want to know*, and *wonder* in a variety of tenses.
> Zaki **wants to know** where we're going.
> I **was wondering** if you wanted to go for a drink sometime.
> Carola**'s been asking** me if we want to go out on Friday.

## Tense change

**D** When reporting questions, we sometimes change the tense (present tense → past tense, *will* → *would*, etc.)

▶ 47.

'Where **does** Emma **live**?' → *He asked me where Emma **lived**.*
'What time **will** you **arrive**?' → *She wanted to know when we'd **arrive**.*

## Word order

E The word order is different from that in direct questions. The subject comes before the verb and you do <u>not</u> use the auxiliary verb *do*. For *yes/no* questions, you use *if* or *whether*.

'Where **does** he **work**?' → *She asked me where **he works**.*
'When **are** we **leaving**?' → *Elsa wants to know when **we're leaving**.*
'**Are** they French?' → *Oliver wondered if **they were** French.*
NOT ~~She asked me where does he work.~~

F We can use *ask*, *want to know*, and *wonder* + *about* + topic.
*Clara **wants to know about** the meeting.*
*Lara **was asking about** our holiday.*

---

**TIP**

We can use *ask for* + noun.
*Kimiko **asked me for** my email address.*
*I **asked for** a pay rise.*
***Did** you **ask for** more time?*

---

# 46 Other reporting verbs (*promise, invite, suggest,* etc.)

A  When we report what someone says we often choose verbs that help us to indicate the nature of what was said. This also helps us to report things from our own point of view and to convey some kind of attitude.

> He **promised** he wouldn't say anything.
> Paula **denied** being involved.
> She **warned** us not to do it.
> Tom**'s suggested** going for a pizza.

B  Reporting verbs take a number of different patterns. Below are some of the most common and useful reporting verbs and their patterns. Note that some verbs occur in more than one pattern.

- Verb + (that-)clause
  Examples include: *admit, agree, claim, complain, confirm, deny, explain, insist, mention, predict, promise, reckon, reveal, say, suggest, think, warn.*

  > She **mentioned that she might be late**.
  > Danny **predicted it would rain**.
  > He **confirmed that he would meet us at the airport**.

- Verb + object + (that-)clause
  Examples include: *assure, convince, inform, promise, reassure, remind, tell, warn.*

  He assured **me** everything was fine.
  **We** were not informed that the meeting was cancelled.

- Verb + to-infinitive
  Examples include: *agree, ask, claim, demand, offer, promise, refuse, threaten, volunteer.*

  Greta **refused to talk** to them.
  Paul **promised not to be** late.

- Verb + object + to-infinitive
  Examples include: *advise, beg, encourage, invite, order, persuade, remind, tell, urge, warn.*

  Lucy persuaded **me** to buy it.
  Can you remind **me** to book the tickets?

- Verb + ing-form
  Examples include: *admit, apologize for, deny, insist on, mention, object to, suggest.*

  She **apologized for being** late.
  He **admitted taking** the money.

- Verb + object + preposition + ing-form
  Examples include: *accuse … of, congratulate … on, talk … into, thank … for, warn … against.*

  I **thanked them for helping** me.

> *She **accused me of lying**.*
> *Jack **talked me into going** with them.*

## Verb + question word

C We can use some reporting verbs with a
  question word (*what*, *why*, etc.) when we
  are not reporting precise information.
  *He **predicted who** would win.*
  ***Did** she **suggest where** to meet?*
  *Vera **didn't mention who** was going.*

## Requests and imperatives

D To report requests and imperatives,
  we use *tell, ask,* or *want* + indirect
  object + to-infinitive.
  *Gregor **told me to phone** him.*
  *He **asked us not to be** late.*
  *Maria **wants me to help** her.*

## Tense change

E When we use a reporting verb that is
  followed by a (that-)clause, we generally
  change the tense (present tense → past
  tense, *will* → *would*, etc.) ▶ 47.
  *'The shower **doesn't work**.' →*
  *I complained that the shower*
  ***didn't work**.*

---

**TIP**

We can use some reporting verbs +
noun.
*He **thanked me for** my help.*
*She **explained the situation**.*
*Petra **apologized for the confusion**.*

---

# 47 Tenses in reporting

**A** When reporting, we generally use the past tense of the reporting verb (*he said ...*, *she told me ...*, etc.) and we change the tense in the clause:

- present tense → past tense
  *'I'm tired.'* → She said she **was** tired.
  *'I **live** in Oxford.'* → She told us she **lived** in Oxford.
  *'It's raining here.'* → He said it **was** raining there.

- past simple / present perfect → past perfect
  *'We **got** lost.'* → She said they'**d got** lost.
  *'I'**ve been** ill.'* → He told us he'**d been** ill.
  *'We'**ve been waiting** for ages.'* → They said they'**d been waiting** for ages.

- will/can/must → would/could/had to
  *'I'll text you.'* → She said she'**d text** me.
  *'I **can't** find it.'* → He said he **couldn't** find it.
  *'We really **must** go.'* → She said they **had to** go.

**B** However, we often use *he said ...*, *she told me ...*, etc. and do not change the tense. This is usually to show or to emphasize that something is still true, relevant, or important.

*'We'll be late.'* → *She said they'll be late.*
*'I **play** the guitar.'* → *He told me he **plays** the guitar.*
*'Tom **arrived** ten minutes ago.'* → *She said Tom **arrived** ten minutes ago.*
*'I **can't** make it tonight.'* → *He said he **can't** make it tonight.*

C  We can also use a reporting verb in the present tense (*he says ...*, *she tells me ...*, etc.). When we use a reporting verb in the present tense, we do <u>not</u> change the tense in the clause.

*'I**'m going out** tonight.'* → *She says she**'s going out** tonight.*
*'She **lives** in New York.'* → *Angela tells me you **live** in New York.*
*'It**'s** a great idea.'* → *Ella thinks that it**'s** a great idea.*
NOT *She says she was going out tonight.*

## Reporting questions and other reporting verbs

D  The same general rules apply for reporting questions (*she asked me ...*, etc.) and for a range of reporting verbs (*he promised ...*, *she insisted ...*, etc.). We most commonly use the reporting verb in the past tense and change the tense in the clause.

*'Where **does** Emma **live**?'* → *He asked me where Emma **lived**.*

47

'**Can** I come with you?' → *He asked if he **could** come with us.*
'Where **shall** I go?' → *She wanted to know where she **should** go.*
'*The shower **doesn't work**.'* → *I complained that the shower **didn't work**.*
'*I **won't be** late, promise.'* → *She promised she **wouldn't be** late.*
'*It's a good idea, believe me.'* → *He convinced me it **was** a good idea.*

E  However, we can also use the reporting verb in the present tense and <u>not</u> change the verb in the clause.

*Tom wants to know who's **going** to the party.*
'*It's a great idea.'* → *She agrees that it's a great idea.*
'*I **broke** the window.'* → *He admits he **broke** the window.'*

---

**TIP**

There is no simple rule about whether or not to change the tense when reporting. The explanations above are useful general rules, and noticing what people say will help you to develop a better understanding.

---

# 48 Introduction to the infinitive

A  An infinitive can be with *to* or without *to*.
> I'd prefer **to go** on Friday.
> I'd rather **go** on Friday.

Whether we use the to-infinitive or the infinitive without *to* depends on the grammatical structure ▶ 49–56.

B  To form the negative, we put *not* before the infinitive.
> I'd prefer **not to go** on Friday.
> I'd rather **not go** on Friday.

## Forms of the infinitive

C  A to-infinitive can have the following forms:

- simple: *to do*
  > I need **to get** a new phone.

- continuous: *to be doing*
  > He appears **to be enjoying** himself.

- perfect: *to have done*
  > I hope **to have finished** by Friday.

- perfect continuous: *to have been doing*
  > It seems **to have been raining**.

The forms of the infinitive without *to* are the same, but without the *to*.
> He let me **leave**.
> I'd rather **be lying** on the beach.

For passive forms of the to-infinitive
▶ 42.

## Infinitive clause

D An infinitive followed by an object,
complement, or adverbial is called an
infinitive clause.

*I don't want **to leave**.*
*I need **to get a new computer**.*
(infinitive + object)
*Jackie seems **to be really nice**.*
(infinitive + complement)
*What's the best way **to get to your
house?*** (infinitive + adverbial)

E When an infinitive clause includes a
preposition, the preposition generally
goes in its normal position, often after
a verb or adjective.

*There are a number of places **to hide in**.*

However, in more formal English the
infinitive clause can begin with the
preposition and a relative pronoun.

*There are a number of places **in which
to hide**.*

## Split infinitive

F We can sometimes put a one-word
adverbial between *to* and the verb. This
is called a 'split infinitive'. Some people
consider this to be incorrect English,
but it is commonly used, especially in
informal contexts and in speaking.

*Our teachers used **to really make** us work hard.*
*I need **to quickly check** my emails.*

## Use of the infinitive

G We use the infinitive:

- to add information to what is expressed by certain verbs, adjectives, and nouns
  *We need **to leave** soon. It was lovely **to see** you. It's time **to go**.*

- to explain the reason, purpose, or function of an action
  *I'm going **to get** some bread. I'm making a poster **to advertise** the college party.*

- as subject or complement
  ***To win** will be unbelievable. The sensible thing is **to wait** here.*

- in certain tense forms
  *He **is to move** to a new job next week.*

H For uses of the to-infinitive ▶ 51–56 and the infinitive without *to* ▶ 49–50.

> **TIP**
>
> In this book, we use the terminology 'to-infinitive' and 'infinitive without *to*' (or 'base form'). However, you may be familiar with other terms, such as 'infinitive with *to*', 'full infinitive', 'bare infinitive', etc.

# 49 Infinitive without *to* (1)

A We use the infinitive without *to* after
the auxiliary verb *do*, after modals, and
after certain verbs.

*What **do** you **want** for lunch?*
*You **must be** here by 6.30.*
*They **made** me **wait** for over half an
hour.*

## After *do*

B We use the infinitive without *to* in
question and negative forms after the
auxiliary verb *do*.

*I **don't like** it.*
*Paul **doesn't drive**.*
***Does** she **live** in Rome?*
***Did** you **read** his book?*
*What **do** you **do**?*

## After modal verbs

C We use the infinitive without *to* after a
modal verb.

*You'**ll be** ok.*
*It **might rain** later.*
*They **should be** here now.*
*I **can play** the piano.*

But note these modal-like phrases
with *to*: *be able to, be allowed to, be
going to, have (got) to,* and *ought to.*

*You **have got to** be joking!*
*You**'re not allowed to** take photos.*
*I **wasn't able to** fix the coffee machine.*

134

### After *had better, would rather*, etc.

D We use the infinitive without *to* after *had better, would rather*, and *rather than*.

*We'd better be going soon.*
*I'd rather get a taxi.*
*Let's take a picnic rather than spend money in a restaurant.*

### After *make, let*, etc.

E We use the infinitive without *to* after *make, let, have*, and *help* + object.

*We made the children clean up.*
*The book made me think.*
*Mr Smith let us leave early.*
*I'll have my assistant contact you next week.*
*Kim helped me tidy up.*

However, we can also use *help* with the to-infinitive and with or without an object.

*Kim helped tidy up.*
*Kim helped to tidy up.*
*Kim helped me to tidy up.*

When we use *make* in the passive, we use the to-infinitive.

*We made the children clean up the mess.*
*The children were made to clean up the mess.*
*They made me wait for ages.*
*I was made to wait for ages.*

## After *see, hear,* etc.

**F** We can use the infinitive without *to* after certain verbs of perception (*see, hear, feel, notice,* etc.) + object.

*Did anyone **see David leave**?*
*I think I **heard a door close**.*

We can also sometimes use the ing-form after these verbs ▶ 67. We use the ing-form to express an extended action or for something in progress. Compare the following sentences:

*I saw the accident **happen**.*
*I saw Jake **playing** football.*

---

### TIP

Here are some more uses of *let* +
infinitive without *to*.
***Let's go*** *for a drink, shall we?*
***Let go!*** *You're hurting me!*
*Will you **let me know** when Daria arrives?*
*Can you **let me have** a copy of the photo?*

For more about *let* ▶ 95.

---

# 50 Infinitive without *to* (2)

A  We use the infinitive without *to* after certain words and structures.

*Why not go by bus?*
*Go and make a coffee, will you?*
*Try and do better next time!*
*Rory's done nothing all day except watch TV.*
*The best thing to do is start again.*

## After *why (not)*

B  We can use the infinitive without *to* after *why* when we are questioning something.

*Why go out if you're feeling so ill?*
*Why get an expensive TV if you hardly ever watch it?*

We often use this structure with *if* or *when*.

*Why bother learning English if you're never going to use it?*
*Why get a taxi when it's only five minutes' walk?*

C  We also use the infinitive without *to* after *why not* when we are making a suggestion. The meaning is similar to *why don't you ...?*

*Why not phone him instead of texting?*
*Why not go by train? It's much quicker.*

# 50

## After *come/go* and ...

**D** When we are making suggestions, giving orders and invitations, and making requests, we can use the expressions *come and* ... and *go and* ... + infinitive without *to*.

> ***Come and have*** *a nice cup of tea.*
> *That box looks heavy. I'll **come and help** you with it.*
> ***Go and see*** *who's at the door, will you?*
> *Could you **go and turn** the TV off if you're not watching it?*

In American English, *and* can be omitted after *come* and *go*.

> ***Go see*** *who's at the door, will you?*

## After *try and* ... , etc.

**E** We can use the infinitive without *to* after *try and* .... This is often when we are making suggestions or giving advice.

> ***Try and be*** *more careful next time.*
> *We'll **try and stay** a bit longer next week.*

We can also use the to-infinitive or gerund after *try*.

> ***Try to be*** *more careful next time.*
> ***Try being*** *more careful next time.*

## After *except* and *but*

**F** We can use the infinitive without *to* after *except* and *but*. In this use *but* has a similar meaning to *except*.

*I'll do anything in the house **except iron**.*
*Lars has done nothing **but complain**
all day.*

## After *do + be*

G We can sometimes use the infinitive
without *to* in cleft sentences with
*do + be*. This is usually when we are
explaining something or making
suggestions.

*All we can **do** is **try** again.*
*The best thing you can **do** is **keep** quiet.*
*The first thing we **did was apologize**
to them.*

We can also use a to-infinitive in this
structure.

*The best thing you can **do is to keep**
quiet.*

---

### TIP

Note that we only use *try and* in the
imperative and with modal verbs.
***Try and** remember.*
*Can you **try and** fix it?*
NOT ~~She tried and fix it.~~
NOT ~~They are trying and renew their visa.~~

*Try to* can be used with other tenses
and without a modal.
*She **tried to** fix it.*
*They **are trying to** renew their visa.*

For more about *try* ▶ 59.

---

51

# 51 Verb (+ object) + to-infinitive

## Verb + to-infinitive

A We use the to-infinitive after certain verbs.

*We're planning to set off after lunch.*
*What time did you arrange to meet?*
*I promise not to tell anyone.*

Some common verbs that are followed by the to-infinitive include: *agree, aim, appear, arrange, ask, attempt, choose, dare, decide, demand, expect, fail, forget, help, hope, intend, learn (how), manage, need, offer, plan, prepare, promise, seem, want, wish* ▶ page 337.

## Verb + object + to-infinitive

B Some verbs that are followed by the to-infinitive must take an object.

*I advise everyone to listen carefully.*
*They persuaded me to go with them.*

Some of the more common and useful verbs include: *advise, allow, ask, beg, cause, challenge, choose, dare, drive, enable, encourage, forbid, force, get, help, inspire, instruct, invite, lead, leave, mean, need, order, pay, permit, persuade, remind, require, teach, tell, tempt, trust, urge, want, warn* ▶ page 338.

The following verbs express thought or attitude and may be rather formal

in use: *assume, believe, consider, expect, feel, find, imagine, know, suppose, suspect, understand.*
  We **believe the allegations to be** *false.*
  I **imagined him to be** *taller.*

## Verbs with or without an object

C We can use some verbs (e.g. *ask, beg, choose, dare, expect, help, need,* and *want*) either with or without an object.
  *He **asked John to leave**.*
  *He **asked to leave**.*
  *What **do** you **want to do**?*
  *What **do** you **want us to do**?*

## Multiple verbs

D We can use one to-infinitive after another.
  *I've decided **to learn to drive**.*
  *Do we need **to pay to get in**?*

## Forms of the infinitive

E We can use different forms of the to-infinitive ▶ 48.
  *I **intend to be sitting** by the pool this time tomorrow.*
  *Jim **hopes to have finished** the report by Friday.*

---

### TIP

There is no rule that tells us which verbs are followed by the to-infinitive. Try to notice and learn them as you come across them.

# 52 Verb + to-infinitive (some patterns)

## *Would like/prefer*, etc.

A We can use *would like/prefer/hate/care* + to-infinitive.

> I **wouldn't like to go** there again.
> I'**d prefer to go** by train.

We can also use *would like/prefer/ hate* + object + to-infinitive.

> I'**d like Katya to come** with us.
> I'**d prefer the taxi to come** a bit earlier.

However, we use *would mind* + gerund.

> **Would** you **mind waiting**?
> NOT *Would you mind to wait?*

Note that we use *would prefer* + to-infinitive, but *would rather* + infinitive without *to* ▶ 49.

> I'**d prefer to go** by train.
> I'**d rather go** by train.

## *Tend, seem, appear*, and *look*

B We use *seem/appear/look/tend* + to-infinitive to sound less direct and to generalize.

> Lou **seems to go** away a lot.
> We **appear to have got lost**!
> Jones **looks to be** a strong contender.
> Jim **tends to finish** work at about 5.30.

We can sometimes omit the verb *to be* after *seem, appear*, and *look*.

*Luke **seems to be** a bit confused.*
OR *Luke **seems** a bit confused.*

The continuous form of *look* can
mean 'aim to'.
> *We **are looking to move** next year.*

### Force, allow, make, and let

C We use *force/allow* + to-infinitive.
> *The police **forced** us **to move** back.*
> *My parents **allowed** me **to stay** up late.*

However, we use *make/let* + infinitive
without *to* ▶ 49.
> *The police **made** us **move** back.*
> *My parents **let** me **stay** up late.*

But we use the to-infinitive when we
use *make* in the passive.
> *We **were made to move** back.*

### Verb phrases

D We use the to-infinitive after certain
verb phrases.
> *We **can't wait to see** you.*
> *I'm **dying to hear** Sophie's news.*
> *You **can't afford to make** mistakes.*
> *He **turned out to be** a fraudster.*

---

**TIP**

Do not use a that-clause with *would
like* or *want*.
**Would** you **like** me to help you?
NOT ~~Would you like that I help you?~~
I **want** you to enjoy yourself.
NOT ~~I want that you enjoy yourself.~~

---

# 53 Adjective + to-infinitive

A We use the to-infinitive after certain
   adjectives.
   *It's **important to be** on time.*
   *I'm **sorry to bother** you, but ….*
   *It's quite **likely to rain** later.*
   *Are you **ready to leave**?*

   The adjectives that we use in this
   way are generally those that express
   personal feelings and attitudes and
   those that express ability, possibility,
   and necessity.

B We use the 'empty subject' *it* in the
   pattern *it* + linking verb + adjective +
   to-infinitive.
   *Is it **possible to use** the computer?*
   *It's **important not to be** late.*
   *It feels **strange to be** here.*
   ***Nice to see** you.* (= It's nice to see you.)

   For more adjectives used in this
   pattern ▶ page 339.

   We also use this pattern with
   adjective phrases.
   *It's **against the law to smoke** in these
   premises.*

C We also use a normal subject (*I*, *we*,
   *Peter*, *the camera*, etc.) + linking verb +
   adjective + to-infinitive.
   ***Peter's willing to help**.*

*The camera is easy to use.*
*I'm surprised to see you here.*
*Pleased to meet you.* (= I'm pleased to meet you.)

For more adjectives used in this pattern ▶ page 339.

D We can use some adjectives in both pattern B and pattern C (e.g. *difficult, easy, free, hard, impossible, right, safe, silly, simple,* and *wrong*).
> *It's easy to use the camera.*
> OR *The camera is easy to use.*
> *Is it safe to drink the water?*
> OR *Is the water safe to drink?*

Some adjectives can only be used in either pattern B or pattern C.
> *Is it possible to use the computer?*
> NOT *Is the computer possible to use?*
> *The coach is ready to leave.*
> NOT *It is ready to leave the coach.*

E We use adjective + *for* + object + to-infinitive when we mention who or what does the action.
> *It's important for everyone to be at the meeting.*
> *Is it possible for you to get here a bit earlier?*
> *It's now almost impossible for Arsenal to win the title.*

**53**

**F** We use adjective + *of* + object + to-infinitive to say what people are like or how they behave.

> It was **kind of him to help**.
> It was **crazy of Alex to do** that.

For more adjectives used in this pattern ▶ page 340.

**G** Note that when we use adjective + *for/of* we use the 'empty subject' *it*. However, we can sometimes begin the sentence with for.

> **For** Arsenal to win the title is now almost impossible.

**H** We use the to-infinitive to express consequence after *enough* or *too* + adjective.

> I'm **too old to take up** skiing.
> Is it **too late to get** a ticket?
> The sea isn't **warm enough to go swimming**.
> Is it a **big enough room to fit** twenty people?

---

### TIP

We use a number of adjectives + to-infinitive to express degrees of probability (e.g. *bound, certain, liable, (un)likely, sure*).
It's **bound to rain** later.
The traffic is **likely to be** bad.
The play is **sure to be** a success.

# 54 Noun + to-infinitive

A We use a to-infinitive after certain
nouns and noun phrases.

*She showed **determination to succeed**.*
*They made **several attempts to climb**
the mountain.*
*I've **no desire to stay** here longer.*
*There's **no need to get** angry.*
*What's **the best way to get** to town?*

For more nouns used in this way ▶ page
340.

B We can use *it + be + noun + to-*
infinitive.

*It's **time to go**.*
*It was **a bad decision not to tell** him.*
*It's **a good idea to get** there early.*
*It would be **a mistake to stay** here.*

C We can use noun + *be* + to-infinitive.
In this pattern we use the to-infinitive
as a complement.

*My **advice is to say** nothing.*
*The **secret is to work** hard at all times.*
*The **important thing is to exercise**
every day and **to eat** healthily.*

D We use noun + *for* + object +
to-infinitive when we mention who
or what does the action.

*It's **time for us to be** going.*
*There's **no need for it to take** so long.*

**E** We use the to-infinitive after an object
to express what needs to happen to
the object.

> *Where are the **documents to translate**?*
> *Have you got much **work to do**?*

**F** We use the pattern *something/anything* +
to-infinitive in requests and suggestions.

> *Is there **anything to eat**?*
> *Take **something to read** on the train.*

**G** We use the to-infinitive to express
consequence after *enough* (*of*) or *too
much/many* (*of*) + noun.

> *Is there **enough time to get** a coffee?*
> *There are **too many of us to go** in
> one car.*

Note that we can leave out the noun
when the meaning is clear.

> *Have you had **enough to eat**?*
> (= enough food to eat)

**H** We use the to-infinitive after *the first,
the second, the last, the only,* etc.

> *Steve's always **the last to arrive**.*
> *She was **the first person to leave**.*

---

### TIP

We can use the to-infinitive as part of
the exclamation *What (a)…!*

*What a place **to live**!*
*What a terrible thing **to say**!*

---

# 55 Question word + to-infinitive

A We can use verb + question word + to-infinitive.
   *I **don't know where to go**.*
   *We **can't decide what to do** this evening.*
   ***Can** you **show** me **how to use** the satnav?*

   For more verbs used in this pattern
   ▶ page 341.

   We do not use *why* + to-infinitive.
   *I don't know why I have to go.*
   NOT *I don't know why to go.*

B We can also use the to-infinitive after words that imply a question word.
   *I don't know **the way to get** to your house.* (= I don't know **how to get** to your house.)
   *Do you know **the best person to contact** about student loans?* (= Do you know **who to contact** about student loans?)

C We can use certain expressions with a question word + to-infinitive.
   *I'm **not sure where to go**.*
   *We've **no idea what to do**.*
   ***Have** you **made up your mind who to invite** to the party?*

Such expressions include: *I've no idea
…, I haven't got a clue …, I'm not sure
…, I've / I haven't made up my mind …,
I couldn't tell you …, Let me know … , I
wonder / am wondering … .*

**D** We can use the above and similar
structures with a noun after the
question words *what, which, whose, how
many,* and *how much.*
   *I can't decide **which tie to wear**.*
   *Let me know **how much food to
   prepare**.*
   *I was wondering **which computer
   to use**?*

**E** We can also use *whether* + to-infinitive
after certain verbs and expressions.
   ***I can't decide whether to go out***
   *tonight or not.*
   ***I'm not sure whether to tell** Beppe
   about the party.*

   We do not use *if* in place of *whether*.
   *I don't know whether to invite Karen.*
   NOT *I don't know if to invite Karen.*

---

**TIP**

We can use a question word + to-
infinitive after some indirect question
phrases (*Could you tell me …?, Do you
know …?, I'd like to know …,* etc.)
*Could you tell me **where to go**?*
*I was wondering **who to speak to** about
my proposal?*

# 56 Other uses of the to-infinitive

## Purpose

**A** We can use a to-infinitive clause to express purpose or the reason for doing something.

*Can I use your phone **to call Tom**?*
*Why are you going out? ~ **To get some milk**.*

We do not use *not* for the negative. Instead, we usually use a structure using *so*.

*Take a map **so you don't get lost**.*
NOT *Take a map not to get lost.*

We do not use *for* with a verb to express purpose.

*I'm going out **to get some money**.*
NOT *I'm going out for get some money.*

## Function

**B** We also use the to-infinitive to explain the function of something.

*You use a protractor **to measure angles**.*
*What's this button for? ~ **To check the power level**.*

**C** We can begin a sentence with the to-infinitive when we want to express how to achieve or obtain something.

***To stay fit**, you should exercise at least twice a week.*

*To survive in this environment,*
*animals need a lot of thick fur.*

We can also begin with *for.*
*For animals to survive in this*
*environment,* they need a lot of thick fur.

## Outcome

**D** We can use a to-infinitive to express an
outcome or result.
*We got to the airport **to discover that**
**the flight was cancelled.***
*He went on **to become a millionaire.***
*I woke up **to find it had been snowing**
**all night.***

We can use *only* before the to-
infinitive to express the idea that
effort has been wasted.
*We raced to the shop **only to find it**
**was closed.***

## As a subject

**E** We can use a to-infinitive or a
to-infinitive clause as a subject.
*ved **To win** would be unbelievable.*
*ved **To solve the problem** should be pretty*
*straightforward.*
*ved **To have loved and lost** is better than*
*not to have loved at all.*

We can often use a gerund instead of
a to-infinitive as a subject ▶ 63.
***Solving the problem** should be pretty*
*straightforward.*

## Comment

F We can use a to-infinitive clause to comment on what follows. We often use it in adverbial phrases such as *to be honest*, *to tell you the truth*, etc.

> **To be honest**, I didn't really enjoy it.
> **To make matters worse**, it rained most of the time.
> **To really annoy you**, I forgot to cancel the order.

G We can use a clause with *to hear*, *to see*, *to watch*, etc. to explain why someone may get the wrong idea.

> **To hear him talk**, you'd think he was some sort of world expert.
> **To watch them play**, you'd never believe they were current champions.

---

### TIP

More formal alternatives to the to-infinitive for expressing purpose or reason are the conjunctions *in order to* and *so as to*.

*You need a lot of training **in order to** be able to use the equipment safely.*

***In order to** get a good seat, it is advisable to check in online.*

*You need to complete the form **so as to** comply with requirements.*

# 57 Introduction to the gerund

**A** The gerund is the ing-form of a verb.

*Do you mind **waiting** here?*
*I love **cooking**.*
***Running** is great exercise.*

For spelling rules for the ing-form
▶ page 332.

**B** To form the negative, we put *not* before the gerund.

*I regret **not going** to the party.*
*Thanks for **not smoking**.*

## Forms of the gerund

**C** A gerund can have the following forms:

- simple: *doing*
  *I enjoy **studying** English.*

- perfect: *having done*
  *He denied **having broken** the window.*

- passive: *being done*
  *I don't like **being lied to**.*

- perfect passive: *having been done*
  *Smith was disappointed at **having been dismissed**.*

## Gerund clause

**D** A gerund followed by an object, complement, or adverbial is called a 'gerund clause'.

*Do you like **playing chess**?*
(gerund + object)
*I really enjoy **being a teacher**.*
(gerund + complement)
*Joe suggested **going to the cinema**.*
(gerund + adverbial)

## Gerund clause with subject

E   A gerund clause can have a subject,
which comes before the gerund. The
gerund clause can act as an object or as
a subject.

*I can't stand **people talking loudly
in public**.*
*I don't remember **you taking this
photo**.*
*Do you mind **me borrowing your
dictionary**?*
***People talking loudly in public**
irritates me.*

In formal contexts, we can sometimes
use a possessive determiner before the
gerund, as the gerund is functioning
as a noun.

*Do you mind **my borrowing** your
dictionary?*
*I'm getting fed up with **Tom's
criticizing**.*

We are more likely to use a possessive
determiner at the beginning of a
sentence.

***Tom's criticizing** is getting annoying.*

> *Your suggesting* we postpone the
> meeting is causing a few problems.

## Uses of the gerund

F  We use the gerund:

- as an object to add information after
  certain verbs
  *I really **enjoy cooking**.*
  *I **can't stand driving** in the city
  centre.*

- after prepositions
  *I'm interested **in going** on the visit.*
  *I ran ten kilometres **without
  stopping**.*

- as a subject or complement
  ***Rowing** is great for keeping fit.*
  *My biggest fear is **failing** at work.*

- to list activities
  *No **running**, **diving**, or **pushing**.*

---

**TIP**

In this book, we use the term 'gerund',
and we use 'ing-form' for the active
participle.
*I love **swimming**.* (gerund)
*I'm **swimming** a kilometre for charity.*
(ing-form / active participle)

However, you may come across
'ing-form' used as a more general
term for both the gerund and the
active participle.

For more about participles ▶ 66–72.

---

# 58 Verb + gerund

A  We use the gerund after certain verbs. The gerund is functioning as the object of the verb. Common verbs that are followed by the gerund include:

- verbs expressing likes and dislikes: *love, like, adore, detest, dislike, don't mind, hate*

    I **love seeing** live music.
    I **don't like driving** in the city centre.

- some verbs with *can't: can't abide, can't bear, can't face, can't help, can't imagine, can't resist, can't stand, can't stop*

    I **can't face ironing** all those shirts.
    I **can't imagine being** a millionaire.

- other verbs: *admit, avoid, (don't) bother, consider, delay, deny, discuss, dread, endure, enjoy, experience, fancy, feel like, finish, imagine, involve, justify, keep (on), mention, (don't) mind, miss, postpone, practise, prefer, quit, recommend, remember, resent, resume, risk, stop, suggest, tolerate*

    Sophie **suggested going** by taxi.
    I **don't feel like cooking**.

- some multi-part verbs: *carry on with, feel up to, get over, give up, look forward to, look into, make up for, put off, put up with*, etc.

*She really should **give up smoking**.*
*I **look forward to meeting** you.*
*Sue**'s looking into going** by train.*
*His visit will **make up for missing**
the match.*

For preposition + gerund ▶ 60–61.
For multi-part verbs ▶ 98–103.

B Some verbs can be followed by a
gerund clause with a subject ▶ 57.
*I don't remember **you buying this
suit**.*
*We discussed **Peter coming with us**.*
*Can you stop **the children going any
further**?*

Some of the more common and useful
verbs with this pattern include: *adore,
can't abide/bear/help/stand, (can't)
imagine, discuss, dislike, hate, involve,
justify, (don't) like, love, (don't) mind,
miss, remember, resent, risk, stop,
tolerate, understand.*

C Note that we can use most of these
verbs with or without a subject in the
gerund clause.
*I **can't imagine my parents being**
**young**.*
*I **can't imagine being** young.*
*I **don't remember you buying** this.*
*I **don't remember buying** this.*

D Note that there are two structures with
   *allow*: *allow* + gerund, and *allow* +
   object + to-infinitive.
   > We **don't allow smoking**.
   > We **don't allow people to smoke**.
   > NOT ~~We don't allow people smoking.~~

## Multiple gerunds

E We can sometimes use one gerund
   after another.
   > As a child, I remember **hating going** to
   > the dentist.

## Forms of the gerund

F We can use different forms of the
   gerund (simple, perfect, etc.) ▶ 57.
   > The protestors risked **being arrested**.
   > Jones admitted **having been** at the
   > scene of the attack.

   We can often use the simple gerund
   and perfect gerund with little
   difference in meaning.
   > I don't remember **meeting** her before.
   > OR I don't remember **having met** her
   > before.

---

### TIP

A useful expression is *be worth* + gerund.
**Is** the film **worth seeing**?
The museum**'s** definitely **worth visiting**.

We also use *be worth* with the 'empty'
subject *it*.
**It's** not **worth waiting**.
**Is it worth visiting** the museum?

---

# 59 Verb + gerund or to-infinitive?

A Some verbs can be followed by either the gerund or the to-infinitive, with little difference in meaning. These verbs include: *begin, can't abide/bear/ stand, cease, commence, continue, intend, love, prefer, propose, start.*

> I **started to learn** English when I was ten.
> OR I **started learning** English when I was ten.
> The situation **continued to improve**.
> OR The situation **continued improving**.

B Note that when the first verb is in the continuous form, it is usually followed by the to-infinitive.

> I'm **beginning to feel** better now.
> We're **intending to leave** before lunch.
> NOT ~~I'm beginning feeling better now.~~

C After *begin, start,* and *continue* we usually use a state verb in the infinitive.

> I **began to understand** the situation.

## Like, love, dislike, hate, etc.

D We use *like, hate,* etc. + gerund to say that we enjoy or don't enjoy something in general.

> I **like driving**.
> I **hate getting up** early.

We use *like, love,* and *hate* +
to-infinitive to say that we think
something is a good or bad idea.
  *I **like to go** for a run at least twice a week.*
  *I **hate to keep** people waiting.*

Note that *would like/love/hate* are
normally followed by the to-infinitive.
  *I'd **like to thank** every one of you.*
  NOT *I'd like thanking every one of you.*

## Try, remember, regret, mean, need, go on

E  We use both the to-infinitive and
gerund after these verbs, but with a
difference in meaning.

  • *remember/forget*

    We use *remember/forget* + gerund to
    talk about memories. We often use
    *forget* with a negative to say we will
    always remember something.
      *Do you **remember meeting** my
      cousins a few years ago?*
      *I'll never **forget going** to India for
      the first time.*

    We use *remember/forget* + to-
    infinitive to say we do or don't
    actually do something.
      *Did you **remember to email** Jenny?*
      *Oh no! I **forgot to book** the table.*
      *Don't **forget to lock** the door.*

- *try*

  We use *try* + gerund when we do something to see what the results will be.

  > I **tried turning** the modem off and on, but the internet still isn't working.

  We use *try* + to-infinitive when we make an effort to achieve something.

  > We **tried to move** the cupboard, but it was too heavy.

- *regret*

  We use *regret* + gerund to say we are sorry about something we did.

  > I really **regret** not **buying** those shoes – they were such a bargain.

  We use *regret* + to-infinitive to announce in advance that we are sorry about something we are going to do. It is usually used in a formal context, and often with verbs such as *inform* or *announce* to give bad news.

  > We **regret to inform** you that your application was not successful.

- *mean*

  We use *mean* + gerund to say that something makes something else necessary or that it involves something.

  > If I take the job, it **means moving** to Cambridge.

We use *mean* + to-infinitive to express intention.

> I **didn't mean to upset** you.

• *need*

We use *need* + gerund with passive meaning. It is the same as *need* + passive infinitive.

> This room **needs decorating**. (= This room needs to be decorated.)

In informal contexts, some people also use *want* + gerund to mean *need*.

> This room **wants decorating**.

We use *need* + to-infinitive to express necessity.

> I **need to get** a new computer.

• *go on*

We use *go on* + gerund to mean continue.

> They **went on talking** for hours.

We use *go on* + to-infinitive to express future developments.

> He dropped out of university, but he **went on to become** one of the world's richest men.

---

**TIP**

We use *stop* + gerund (**Stop worrying** about it.). However, we also use *stop* with the to-infinitive to express reason or purpose (We **stopped to get** some petrol on the way here.) ▶ 48.

---

163

# 60 Preposition + gerund (1)

**A** We use the gerund after prepositions.

*This button is **for checking** the power levels.*

*I ran ten kilometres **without stopping**.*

*He put on weight as a result **of not exercising**.*

We do not use an infinitive after a preposition.

NOT *This button is for check the power levels.*

NOT *This button is for to check the power levels.*

For verb/adjective/noun + preposition + gerund ▶ 61.

**B** Prepositions that can be followed by the gerund include: *against, besides, by, despite, for, from, in, on, through, with, without*.

*They managed to win **despite having** only nine players.*

***Besides being** a top lawyer, she also writes novels.*

*I'm **against hunting** foxes.*

**C** Some common uses of preposition + gerund include:

• *without*

We use *without* + gerund to say that we don't do something, or something isn't done.

*I translated everything **without using** a dictionary.*
*She left **without saying** goodbye.*

- *by*

We use *by* + gerund to say how something happens.

*They got into the house **by breaking** a downstairs window.*
*The thieves escaped **by jumping** into the next door garden.*

- *for*

We use *for* + gerund to say what we use something for.

*That cloth is **for cleaning** the windows.*
*What's this for? ~ It's **for draining** pasta.*

- *on*

We use *on* + gerund to mean 'as soon as'.

***On entering** the room, I got the shock of my life.*
*James apologized immediately **on realizing** his mistake.*

- *in*

We use *in* + gerund to mean 'as a result of'.

***In offering** online ordering, the company trebled sales in the first six months.*

60

**D** There are many preposition expressions that are followed by the gerund. Common and useful ones include: *as a result of, as for, as well as, because of, by means of, far from, how about, in addition to, in favour of, in spite of, in the process of, instead of, on account of, on the point/verge of, what about.*

> We're **on the verge of making** an important breakthrough.
> Shall we eat out this evening **instead of cooking** something?

**E** With some prepositions and preposition expressions we can use a subject before the gerund.

> **Besides Katie being** a top lawyer, she also writes novels.
> I'm 100% **against people smoking** in public places.
> **Instead of us coming** to you, why don't you come and stay with us?

---

### TIP

There are many different prepositions and many different uses. When you see a preposition followed by a gerund, make a note of the pattern. Try to make other sentences using the same pattern.

# 61 Preposition + gerund (2)

A We sometimes use a gerund after prepositional verbs and after collocations of adjective/noun + preposition.

*We're **thinking of moving** house.*
*Are you **interested in coming** with us?*
*There was a **delay in sending** the package.*

B We use a gerund after prepositional verbs (e.g. *admit to, apologize for, concentrate on, depend on*). For a list of these verbs ▶ 341.

*Jack **insisted on paying** for the coffees.*
***Did** they **apologize for being** late?*
*I **object to being spoken to** in that manner.*

C Some prepositional verbs must have an object (e.g. *accuse someone of, congratulate someone on, thank someone for*). For a list of these verbs ▶ 342.

*They **accused me of lying**!*
*My parents **discouraged me from joining** the army.*
*I'd like to **thank everyone for helping** me these past few days.*

**D** We use a gerund after some adjectives + preposition (e.g. *afraid of, famous for, serious about*). For a list of these adjectives ▶ 343.

*Are you **serious about moving** to Australia?*
*I'm really **sorry for being** late.*
*I'm not **used to driving** on the left.*

**E** We use a gerund after some nouns + preposition. The most common prepositions used after a noun are *of* (e.g. *chance of, memories of, way of*) and *in* (e.g. *difficulty in, interest in, pleasure in*).

*I've got lots of wonderful **memories of living** in Kenya.*
*He took much **pleasure in reading** aloud to his wife.*

Other common and useful noun + preposition patterns include: *advantage of/to/in, alternative to, comparison between, credit for, delay in, difference between, information about, point in/of, reaction to, reason for, success in, trouble with, use in.*

*Is there an **alternative to going** by bus?*
*I've got some **information about joining** the library.*

For more nouns + preposition used with the gerund ▶ 344.

Note that some nouns can be used with different prepositions.

*What's the **use of/in getting** a car if you can't drive?*

*There's no **advantage to/in arriving** early.*

F After a preposition, we sometimes use a gerund clause with a subject ▶ 57.

*I **object to people smoking** in restaurants.*

*I'm so **pleased about Sandra getting** accepted at Harvard.*

*There's a lot of strong **reaction to Smith becoming** President.*

---

### TIP

*Look forward to* is a common and useful expression that is followed by the gerund.

*We're really **looking forward to seeing** you.*

*I'm **looking forward to going** home!*

We can also use *look forward to* + noun.

*I'm so **looking forward to my holiday**!*

*Are you **looking forward to the party**?*

---

# 62 Preposition + gerund or to-infinitive?

**A** After some verbs and adjectives we can use either a preposition + gerund or a preposition + to-infinitive, and there is generally no difference in meaning.

I **voted for carrying on** without a break.
OR I **voted to carry on** without a break.
He's **afraid of making** a mistake.
OR He's **afraid to make** a mistake.
I'm **sorry for being** such a nuisance.
OR I'm **sorry to be** such a nuisance.

For more verbs and adjectives used in this way ▶ pages 341–2.

**B** After other verbs and adjectives with which we can use either a preposition + gerund or a preposition + to-infinitive, there <u>is</u> a difference in meaning.
Here are some examples.

I **don't agree with banning** mobile phones in restaurants. (general opinion)
We **agreed to meet** at six-thirty. (specific arrangement)
She's **anxious about meeting** him. (She's worried/nervous about meeting him.)
She's **anxious to meet** him. (She really wants to meet him.)
I'm **sorry for losing** your camera. (I apologize that I lost your camera.)

*I'm **sorry to tell** you that you didn't
get the job.* (I regret that I have to
tell you …)
*Are you **sure about going** by bus?* (Are
you sure going by bus is a good idea?)
*She's **sure to be** late.* (I'm sure she will
be late.)
*Are you **OK about leaving** at 6.30?*
(Are you happy about leaving at 6.30?)
*Are you **OK to leave** at 6.30?* (Is it
possible for you to leave at 6.30?)

C Some verbs, adjectives, and nouns are
followed by *to* + gerund.
   *No one **admitted to telling** her.*
   *Jones **confessed to committing** over
   20 offences.*
   *He is **resigned to working** late.*
   *I have no **objection to meeting** again
   next week.*
   *What was Gerta's **reaction to hearing**
   the news?*

### TIP

*Be/get used to* + gerund is a useful
expression to say that we are, or we are
becoming, familiar with something.
*I'm **not used to driving** on the left.*
*Are you **getting used to speaking** English?*

# 63

# 63 Gerund as subject, object, and complement

## Gerund as subject

A We can use a gerund or a gerund clause as a subject. This is when the subject is an activity or action.

**Swimming** is great for fitness.
**Eating chocolate** makes me happy.
**Finishing the report by Friday** won't be easy.

## It + be + gerund

B Sometimes we can use *it* as the subject instead of a gerund clause. When we do this, the gerund clause goes at the end.

**Talking to him** is a waste of time.
OR It's a waste of time **talking to him**.

Useful expressions that have these patterns include: *no use/good, a waste of time/money, (not) worth, an experience, fun, a nuisance, a pain*

**Getting a taxi** is a complete waste of money.
OR It's a complete waste of money **getting a taxi**.
**Saying sorry** is no good. It's too late.
OR It's no good **saying sorry**. It's too late.
**Is it worth reading** the Darren Shan books?
OR Are the Darren Shan books **worth reading**?

## Gerund as object

C A gerund or gerund clause can
   function as the object of a verb ▶ 57, 58.

   *I love **cooking**.*

   *Luke's given up **eating meat**.*

   *I don't like **driving at night**.*

## Gerund as a complement

D We can use a gerund or a gerund
   clause as a complement after *be* in
   focusing phrases such as *what I
   remember is ...*, *my earliest memory
   is ...*, etc. We use the gerund when the
   complement is an activity or action.

   *What I remember most is **walking
   along the beach**.*

   *My biggest regret is **not working
   harder at school**.*

   We can also use the pattern *It's ...
   that ...* .

   *It's **walking along the beach** that I
   remember most.*

---

### TIP

We can also sometimes use the
to-infinitive as a subject, but this is less
common than using the gerund ▶ 56.
**Finishing the report by Friday** won't
be easy.
**To finish the report by Friday** won't
be easy.

---

# 64 Other patterns with the gerund

A There are a number of expressions that are followed by a gerund or gerund clause. Some common and useful ones include:

- expressions with (*no*) *point/use*
  **There's no point/use (in) waiting** any longer. Let's go.
  **It's no use talking** to him. He won't listen.
  **What's the point of getting** a car if you can't drive?
  **What's the use in earning** a lot of money if you never spend it?

- *have fun/difficulty/a hard time/trouble/problem(s)*, etc.
  We **had fun working** together.
  Did you **have any problems getting here**?

- *there is a problem/difficulty/delay (in)/an issue*, etc.
  **There was a** slight **problem getting** into the office.
  **There might be a delay in getting** tickets.

B We use a gerund after *than*, *like*, and *as … as* when we express comparison or similarity.

*Not many things are better for you*
***than running**.*
*That film was **like watching** paint dry!*
*Is the bus **as** quick **as going** by train?*

C We use *prefer* + gerund to express
general preferences.
*I like skiing, but I **prefer snowboarding**.*

We use *prefer* + gerund + *to* + gerund
when we express a preference for one
activity over another.
*I prefer **snowboarding to skiing**.*

Note that we use (*would*) *prefer* + to-
infinitive to express preference on a
particular occasion.
*Shall we drive? ~ I'd **prefer to walk**.*

D We use *how/what about* + gerund to
make suggestions.
***How about eating out** this evening?*
***What about not going away** this
weekend and just **staying** at home for
a change?*

Note that we can also use *how/what
about* followed by a subject clause.
***How about we eat out** this evening?*

---

**TIP**

We often use gerunds when we are
listing activities. The following is from a
noticeboard at a swimming pool.

*The following are not allowed:*
*diving   running   shouting*

---

## 65

# 65 Determiner + gerund

A  We can sometimes use a determiner such as *the* before a gerund.
   *My new job's OK, but I don't like **the commuting**.*
   ***The not knowing** is the hardest part.*

   We use *the* to express specific activity. We use the gerund without *the* to express more general ideas. Compare the following sentences.
   *I don't like **the commuting**.*
   (commuting as part of this job)
   *I don't like **commuting**.* (commuting in general)

B  We use *do the* + gerund for some types of work, especially for routine housework.
   *I usually **do the cleaning** on Saturdays.*
   *Have you **done the washing** yet?*

C  We can use different determiners with a gerund, for example *this, that, some, no, a lot of, a little, a bit of, much.*
   *I need to do **some ironing**.*
   ***This digging** is hard work!*
   *Is there **much tidying up** to do?*

   We can use *all this* and *all that* for emphasis.
   ***All this arguing** is not helping the situation.*

We can also use a possessive noun or adjective.

*Jason's playing is getting much better.*
*His singing is getting on my nerves.*
*Their constant disagreeing has got to stop!*

D We can sometimes use the pattern *the* + gerund + *of* + object. It is generally rather formal, and is typically used in official, written contexts.

*The taking of photographs is prohibited.*
*The campaign promoted the eating of healthy foods.*

Note that we often use a noun rather than the gerund.

*The education of women is still an issue in some countries.*
OR *The educating of women is still an issue in some countries.*
*Some think that the sale of bonds is beneficial.*
OR *Some think that the selling of bonds is beneficial.*

---

**TIP**

The gerund is never plural.
*Their dancing is very good.*
*There's a lot of washing to do.*
NOT *Their dancings are very good.*
NOT *There are a lot of washings to do.*

---

# 66 Introduction to participles

A There are three different types of participle: the active participle (also called the 'present participle'), the past participle, and the passive participle.

B The active participle is the ing-form of a verb.
   *I'm **sending** an email.*
   *I saw Jim **waiting** for a bus.*

   For spelling rules of the ing-form of verbs ▶ page 332.

C The form of the past participle depends on whether the verb is regular or irregular.

   For regular verbs, the past participle is verb + *-ed* ▶ page 331.
   *I've **worked** here for ten years.*

   For irregular verbs there are a number of different forms/endings ▶ page 329.
   *We've **made** good progress with the report.*

D The passive participle has the same form as the past participle. It is usually used with *be* to form passive structures.
   *The first World Cup **was held** in Uruguay.*
   *The rings **were made** in the 16th century.*

However, it can also be used with *get*
and *have* ▶ 40, or *need*.
*I must **get** my hair **cut**.*
*We **need** this letter **translated**.*

E  To form the negative, we put *not*
before the participle.
*I listened, **not understanding** a word
he said.*
***Not selected** for the team, Jones
watched from the sidelines.*

F  Active and past participles are used
with *be* or *have* to form continuous
and perfect tenses:

- continuous: *be* + active participle
  *I'm **making** a coffee.*

- perfect: *have* + past participle
  *I've **made** a big mistake.*

## Other forms of the participle

G  As well as the three main participles
(active, past, and passive), there are
three other forms of the participle:

- perfect participle: *having done*
  ***Having missed** the bus, she arrived
  late for work.*

- perfect passive participle: *having
  been done*
  ***Having been delayed** twice, the
  flight finally left at midnight.*

• continuous passive participle:
*being done*
> We saw many shops **being looted** in
> the riots.

## Participle clause

H A participle followed by an object,
complement, or adverbial is called a
participle clause.

> *I can hear someone **playing music**.*
> (participle + object)
> ***Living alone**, Jim always welcomed
> visitors.* (participle + complement)
> *I saw Jenny **walking along the beach**.*
> (participle + adverbial)

A participle clause can have a subject.
> ***The weather being** fine, they went for
> a walk.*
> ***Margaret not being** at the meeting
> caused a few problems.*

## Patterns with participles

I We use a participle:

• before nouns ▶ 72
> *It's a long **winding** road.*
> *Be careful of the **broken** bottle.*
> *There was a **deafening** silence.*

• after certain verbs ▶ 67
> *I **saw** Jo **walking** past the park.*
> *I **didn't notice** Jack **leaving**.*
> *I **found** a dog **running** wild.*

- after certain conjunctions ▸ 68, 71

    *Can you turn off the lights **before leaving**?*

    *Smith was sent off two minutes **after scoring**.*

- as prepositions ▸ 71

    ***Following** lunch, there'll be a quick presentation.*

    ***Considering** all the risks, the trip went very well.*

- in clauses of time, reason, result, and condition ▸ 68, 69

    ***Arriving** home, she began to prepare the meal for the evening.*

    ***Not having** a map, we relied on the direction of the sun.*

    *The team played really well, **winning** 3–0.*

    *Weather **permitting**, we'll leave tomorrow.*

- in shortened relative clauses ▸ 70

    *Zara's the girl **standing** next to the door.*

    *We stayed in a room **overlooking** the sea.*

---

**TIP**

It is often not clear whether an ing-form of a verb is a present participle or a gerund; in fact, experts often do not agree. The important thing is to make sure you use them correctly and not to worry about the terminology.

# 67 Verb + object + participle

## Active participles

**A** We can use an object + active participle after a verb of perception such as *feel, hear, listen to, notice, observe, overhear, see, sense, smell,* and *watch*.

>I can **smell something burning**.
>I **saw Andy waiting** for a bus.
>Can you **hear someone playing** the piano?

**B** We can also use a verb of perception + object + infinitive without *to*. We use this pattern to express a complete action.

>Did you **see anyone take** my bag?
>I didn't **notice Jack leave** the party.

*Smell* cannot be used with object + infinitive without *to*.

>NOT ~~I can smell something burn.~~

**C** Note that we can often use either pattern (infinitive without *to* or active participle) with a different emphasis or focus.

>We **watched Kim play** football this morning. (focus on the complete activity)
>We **watched Kim playing** football this morning. (focus on the activity in progress)

182

**D** We can use an object + active participle after a few verbs which aren't verbs of perception. These include *catch*, *find*, *get*, *have*, *keep*, *leave*, and *start*.

> They **kept us waiting** for ages.
> They **caught the prisoner trying** to escape.
> I went to bed and **left them chatting**.
> I finally **got the internet working** again.
> They **had the flag flying** by midday.

Unlike with verbs of perception, we cannot use these verbs with object + infinitive without *to*.

> NOT ~~They kept us wait for ages.~~

**E** We can also use *spend/waste/lose* + amount of time/money + active participle.

> They **spent ten million euros modernizing** the offices.
> I **wasted an hour looking** for the file.

## Passive participles

**F** We can use object + passive participle after:

- a verb of perception
  > We **saw people arrested**. (focus on the complete action)
  > We **saw people being arrested**. (focus on the activity in progress)

- a few verbs which aren't verbs of perception, such as *discover*, *find*, *get*, *have*, and *leave*

67

The police **discovered the painting hidden** behind a false wall.

- verbs expressing likes and desires, such as *hate*, *(would) like*, *love*, *need*, *prefer*, and *want*

  We'**d like the interviews held** as soon as possible.

We can also use *to be* + participle.

  We'**d like the interviews to be held** as soon as possible.

## Passive verb + participle

G We can use passive verb + active or passive participle for a few verbs. These include *hear*, *observe*, *see*, *catch*, *discover*, *find*, *keep*, and *leave*.

  The prisoner **was caught trying** to escape.

  The painting **was discovered hidden** behind a false wall.

---

**TIP**

A useful expression that uses verb + object + active participle is *I saw you/ him*, etc. + *-ing*.

**I saw you waiting** for the bus this morning.

**I saw him coming** out of the supermarket.

Another useful expression is this apology.

Sorry to **keep you waiting**.

---

# 68 Participle clauses (time)

A We can use an active participle clause when two events happen at the same time.

*Joe's in the kitchen **making a coffee**.*
*I fell asleep **watching TV last night**.*
*I hurt my knee **playing rugby**.*
(= I hurt my knee while I was playing rugby.)

The active participle clause can sometimes come first. This is mainly used in writing and in some literary contexts.

***Driving to work**, James noticed something strange.*

B We can also use an active participle clause for an event that is immediately followed by another connected event. The participle clause always comes first and, as above, this pattern is usually used in writing and is less common in speech.

***Arriving home**, they realized they had left the photo at Jack's house.*
***Reaching the end of the road**, they turned back.*
NOT ~~They realized they had left the photo at Jack's house, arriving home.~~

We can use a perfect participle to emphasize that the first event is completed before the second, or when there is a time interval between the two events.

*Having arrived home, they realized they had left the photo at Jack's house.*

*Having lost all their last five games, the Blues dropped to tenth in the table.*

C We can use an active participle after the time conjunctions *after, before, following, once, since, until, when, whenever,* and *while.* This is more usual in more formal contexts such as writing.

*Can you turn off the lights before leaving?*

*You must wear protective goggles when using power tools.*

*After meeting the French President, Mr Brown headed for Brussels.*

*Please check your order before confirming payment.*

*He's worked here since leaving school.*

In general speech we are more likely to use a subject and finite verb.

*Can you turn off the lights before you leave?*

*Please check your order before you confirm payment.*

*He's worked here since he left school.*

Note that we use a time conjunction + participle only when the person or thing is the same in both clauses.

*After meeting* the French President, Mr Brown headed for Brussels.
(= After Mr Brown met the French President, …)
Tina's been interested in opera *since* first *hearing* 'Nessun dorma'.
(= … since Tina first heard 'Nessun dorma')

D   We can use a passive participle in all of the uses above.

Sarah is in the living room *being measured* for her wedding dress.
It's hard to concentrate while *being forced* to listen to that music!
Once *opened*, the contents should be eaten within one week.

### TIP

A common and useful pattern is *be busy* + active participle.
Jim*'s busy doing* some work.
I*'ll be busy preparing* for the conference this afternoon.

# 69 Participle clauses (reason, result, condition)

## Reason

A We can use an active participle clause to express reason. This is only when the person or thing is the same in both clauses. This structure is mainly used in more formal contexts such as writing.

*Feeling unwell*, Lara went to bed.
*Needing to reach agreement*, the ministers talked all night.
They walked home, *not having money for a taxi*.

The clause includes the sense 'because'.
*Not knowing the area*, we got lost.
(= Because we didn't know the area, we got lost.)

B We can use a perfect participle to emphasize that the first event is completed before the second.
*Having missed the bus*, he was late for work.
*Not having seen each other for years*, they had a lot of catching up to do.
*Having won best actor Oscar*, she now commands up to $20 million a film.

C We can also use a subject before a participle; this is usually only in more formal contexts.

*The weather improving, we are seeing more spring flowers.*

However, we can use *with* to make the sentence sound less formal.

**With the weather improving**, *we are seeing more spring flowers.*

*I can't concentrate **with you making all that noise.***

## Result

D We can use an active participle clause to express result.

*The team played really well, **winning 3–0**.*

*The winds gusted up to 120 mph, **causing damage to hundreds of houses**.*

## Condition

E We can use an active participle clause to express a condition. We can use a subject before the participle.

*I'll get two tickets, **assuming they've got some left**.*

*We'll stop for a coffee on the way, **time permitting**.*

***Weather permitting**, the match will resume at 1.30.*

The meaning is similar to *if* or *on the condition that*.

*We'll have a barbecue, **weather permitting**.* (= … if the weather permits it.)

F We can use a form of passive participle in all of the uses above.

*The lecture being cancelled*, we had the afternoon off.

*Woken* by the noise, Toby jumped out of bed.

*Not having been looked after*, the house fell into disrepair.

The team played really badly, *being beaten* 3–0.

*Having been awarded* best actor Oscar, she now commands up to $20 million a film.

Wrongly *imprisoned*, he was freed after five years.

G We can also use the passive participle to state facts.

*Held* every four years, the Olympics are the world's greatest sporting event.

---

**TIP**

A lot of these patterns can sound very formal, so be careful when you use them. In most situations it may be better to use conjunctions such as *as*, *because*, *so*, *and*, and *if* and a finite clause.

They walked home **because they didn't have money for a taxi.**

I'll get two tickets **if they've got some left.**

**She was feeling unwell so** she went to bed.

# 70 Participles in relative clauses

A A relative clause follows a noun or noun phrase. It identifies the noun/noun phrase or adds information. Relative clauses can be full (*Do you know the guy **who is talking to Jim**?*) or shortened (*Do you know the guy **talking to Jim**?*). (Shortened relative clauses are also known as 'reduced relative clauses'.)

We use participles in shortened relative clauses.

*Zara's the girl **standing** next to the door.*
*Bags **left** unattended will be removed.*

B When in the full relative clause the relative pronoun (*who, which, that,* etc.) is followed by the verb *be*, we can usually omit *be* and the relative pronoun to form the shortened clause. This happens with:

• continuous tenses
  *Zara's the girl **standing** next to the door.* (= Zara's the girl who is standing next to the door.)
  *Who were the people **talking** to Jo?*
  *The number of students **living** in the area has increased.*
  *What's the name of the person **meeting** us at the airport tomorrow?*

- the passive

**Bags left unattended** *will be removed.* (= Bags which are left unattended will be removed.)

*They've found the money* **stolen in the robbery**.

*The number of homes* **rented by students** *has increased.*

*The houses* **being built on James Street** *look interesting.*

Note that the participle can refer to the present, past, or future.

C We can sometimes use an active participle in place of a relative pronoun + simple tense. This is when we express a fact, state, or permanent situation.

*The people* **living next door** *are students.* (= The people who live next door are students.)

*We stayed in a room* **overlooking the beach**.

*Anyone* **finishing in the top three** *gets a medal.*

*Fans* **wanting the best seats** *started queuing early.*

We do not use an active participle for a single complete action.

*The lion* **which escaped** *is said to be highly dangerous.*

NOT *The lion escaping is said to be highly dangerous.*

**D** We can use a shortened relative clause after *there is/are*, etc.

*There are six of us **going on the visit**.*
(= There are six of us who are going on the visit.)
*There are three people **working in the office**.*
*Are there many students **living near you**?*

**E** An adding relative clause (also known as a 'non-defining relative clause') adds information to the noun/noun phrase. In adding relative clauses, we can use an active participle in place of a relative pronoun + simple tense when something is the result of something else.

*Joe Evans won $215 million, **making him one of the USA's richest people overnight**.* (= Joe Evans won $215 million, which made him one of the USA's richest people overnight.)

---

**TIP**

We often use participles when we describe things.
*It's a small black bag **covered in sequins**.*
*It's a statue of a woman **holding a torch, standing in New York harbour**.*

# 71 Other patterns with participles

**A** We can use a participle after verbs such as *go*, *lie*, *run*, *sit*, and *stand* to express two actions that happen at the same time.

*Onlookers **stood watching** the fire.*
*We **stood pressed** against the stage.*
*Everyone **ran screaming** from the building.*

We often put an adverbial or adjective between the verb and participle.

*I **sat on the sofa reading** my book.*
*He **lay still trying** not to be seen.*

**B** We can use *go* + active participle for some leisure activities that we go somewhere to do.

*Let's **go fishing**.*
*We **went camping** last weekend.*

**C** We use *with* + subject + participle to add detail to something. It is often used in more formal contexts, such as news reports.

*The conference was a great success, **with people coming** from all over Europe.*
*The storm destroyed hundreds of homes, **with thousands made** homeless.*

**D** We can use an active or passive
participle after some conjunctions
such as *although*, *once*, *if*, and *unless*.
　**Although being** *from a wealthy family,*
　*I was sent to the local school.*
　*Truffles are much tastier **if eaten**
　within a few days of being picked.*
　***Once bitten**, twice shy.*

We also use participles after some
time conjunctions ▶ 68.

**E** There are a number of common
expressions and idioms that include
an active participle. Some useful ones
include: *all being well, concerning,
considering, following, judging by/
from, providing, regarding, supposing,
talking of.*
　***All being well**, we'll arrive around noon.*
　***Providing** it doesn't rain, we'll have
　the reception in the garden.*
　***Judging from** his mood, I'd guess he's
　had some bad news.*
　***Talking of** Karen, did you hear she's
　getting married?*

---

**TIP**

There are a number of useful
expressions with *speaking*.
***Generally speaking**, we finish work at
about 6.30.*
***Broadly speaking**, men can't multitask.*
***Strictly speaking**, you should wear a tie.*
***Frankly speaking**, I'm not that impressed.*

# 72 Participles as adjectives

### *Interested* or *interesting*? etc.

A Some participles can function like adjectives.

- We use some past participles to express how we feel about something.

  *I'm not **interested** in football.*
  *You must be **excited** about your holiday.*
  *I'm pretty **relaxed** after that swim.*

- We use some active participles to talk about the thing or person that causes the feelings.

  *Football isn't **interesting**.*
  *Your holiday sounds very **exciting**.*
  *That swim was pretty **relaxing**.*

For a list of verbs that we can use as adjectives in this way ▶ page 345.

### Participle + noun

B We can use some active and past participles before a noun. The participle functions like an adjective.

  *That was a pretty **relaxing swim**.*
  *There's no **running water**.*
  *There were several **broken windows**.*

Passive participles as adjectives describe the result of an action.

  *Most **stolen cars** are never found.*
  *(= cars which have been stolen)*

*The **edited report** was much shorter.*
(= the report which had been edited)

Past participles as adjectives do not have passive meaning.
*The road was blocked by a **fallen tree**.*
(= a tree which had fallen)
*The **escaped lion** is said to be highly dangerous.* (= the lion which has escaped)

## Modifying a participle

C We can modify a participle in a number of ways.

- We can sometimes use a prefix (*re-*, *mis-*, *un-*, etc.) with a participle.
  *an **unforgiving** situation an **unresolved** issue a **misspent** youth a **recurring** problem*

  Sometimes we cannot use the prefix with the verb.
  NOT *I misspent my youth.*
  NOT *I unforgive you.*

- We can sometimes use an adverb with a participle.
  ***rapidly fading** light **recently broken** windows a **rarely seen** sight a **much-loved** actor a **much-travelled** road.*

• We can form compound participles.
*tasty-looking* food  a *south-facing*
room  **purpose-built** offices  a **time-saving** device

Note we do not use participle clauses
before nouns.

Most cars **stolen by professional thieves** are never found.
NOT ~~Most stolen by professional thieves cars are never found.~~

D We can add *-ed* to some nouns to
make them function like a participial
adjective.
*a **gated** property* (= a property which
you enter through a gate)

This is most common with compounds.
*a **broad-minded** person*
*a **long-haired** hippy*
*a **bad-tempered** old woman*

---

**TIP**

It is sometimes not easy to know
whether a participle can be used
before a noun. For example we can
say *sleeping children*, but not *playing
children*; and we can say *an unresolved
problem*, but not *a discussed problem*.
It is important to notice which
participles are used in which way.

---

# 73 Introduction to modal verbs

## Form

A  The modal verbs are *can*, *could*, *must*, *might*, *may*, *should*, *would*, *will*, and *shall*.

A modal verb always has the same form and the ending never changes to -*s*, -*ing*, or -*ed*.
*He can speak several languages.*
NOT *He cans speak several languages.*

B  After a modal verb, we use the infinitive of the verb without *to*.
*We **can park** here.*
*I **must go** now.*
*It **might rain** later.*
*He **should arrive** by midnight.*

We can also use the continuous infinitive (e.g. *be doing*, *be working*) or passive infinitive (e.g. *be done*, *be finished*).
*The internet **should be working** again now.*
*I **must be going** in a few minutes.*
*The report **must be submitted** by the end of the week.*
*The gallery **will be opened** by the President.*

**C** To form a negative, we use modal verb + *not* or *-n't*.

> It **might not** rain later.
> I **mustn't** be late.
> We **can't** park here.
> You **shouldn't** be doing that.

We do not use *don't/doesn't* to form a negative.

NOT ~~We don't can park here.~~

**D** To form a question, we put the modal verb before the subject.

> **Can we** buy tickets in advance?
> **Shall I** wait for you?
> **Could you** help me for a minute?

We do not use *do* to form a question.

NOT ~~Do we can buy tickets in advance?~~

**E** To form the past tense, we use modal + perfect infinitive (e.g. *have done*, *have finished*).

> They **should have arrived** ten minutes ago.
> He **could've got lost**.
> Stefan **might not have been listening** when the announcement was made.

The exception to this is that *could(n't)* is the past tense for most uses of *can('t)*.

> I **could** ride a bike when I was three.
> NOT ~~I can have ridden a bike when I was three.~~

For the use of *can't have* ▶ 78.

F Some verbs are semi-modal verbs. This is because they have properties of both modal verbs and ordinary verbs. The semi-modal verbs are *ought to*, *have (got) to*, *need to*, and *had better* ▶ 84.

> We **ought to leave** soon.
> I've **got to see** Dr Boyle.
> You'**d better not be** late.

## Use

G We use modal verbs to express ideas such as ability, obligation, permission, and possibility.

> He **can** *swim.* (ability)
> You **must** *listen carefully.* (obligation)
> **Can** *we park here?* (permission)
> We **might** *be a bit late.* (possibility)

---

### TIP

Most modal verbs have more than one use and meaning. For example:
**Can** *you play the piano?* (ability)
**Can** *you lend me ten pounds?* (possibility)
*You* **must** *arrive on time.* (obligation)
*My keys* **must** *be here somewhere!* (deduction)
Make sure you understand these different uses and meanings.

---

# 74 *Can, could,* and *be able to* (ability)

## *Can*

A We use *can* and *can't* to talk about general abilities and skills.

> Peter **can** speak a little Japanese.
> I **can't** play any musical instruments.
> **Can** you ski? ~ No, I **can't**. **Can** you?
> The telescope **can** see billions of light years into space.

B We also use *can* and *can't* to talk about ability at a particular time.

> Do you think you **can** fix it?
> I **can't** read this – the writing's too small.

## *Could*

C We use *could* and *couldn't* as the past tense of *can* and *can't* when expressing ability in the past.

> My grandfather **could** speak five languages.
> **Could** dinosaurs climb trees?
> I **couldn't** swim until I was about eight.
> I **couldn't** fix the problem, I'm afraid.
> The first cars **could** travel at only a few miles per hour.

## *Can/could* or *be able to*

D We can sometimes use *be able to* instead of *can* or *could* to talk about ability in the present or past. This is generally less

common than using *can* or *could* and is
usually in more formal contexts.

*Crocodiles **are able to** go without food
for up to six months.*

*I **am not able to** attend the meeting,
I'm afraid.*

*The telescope **is able to** see billions of
light years into space.*

*I **wasn't able to** swim until I was
about eight.*

*The first telescopes **were able to** see
only a few hundred metres.*

E  However, we use *was/were able to* and
<u>not</u> *could* to talk about a particular
situation in the past when the meaning
is 'managed' or 'succeeded'.

*Ten-man Rotherham United **were able
to** hold on to draw against Oxford.*

*The question is: how **were** the prisoners
**able to** escape?*

NOT ~~Ten-man Rotherham United
could hold on to draw against Oxford.~~

F  When the meaning is 'didn't manage'
or 'didn't succeed' we can usually
use either *wasn't/weren't able to* or
*couldn't*. In informal contexts such as
in conversation, *couldn't* is generally
more common.

*Rotherham **weren't able to** hold on
against Oxford.*

*Rotherham **couldn't** hold on against
Oxford.*

## 74

### Be able to – other tenses

G We use *be able to* and <u>not</u> *can* or *could* in other tenses and forms:

- with *will*

    You'**ll be able to** speak reasonable French after a few lessons.
    In the future, humans **will be able to** communicate with animals.
    **Will** you **be able to** fix the problem?

- in a perfect tense

    I'**ve been able to** ski since I was four.
    Have long **have** you **been able to** ride a motorbike?

- after certain verbs, nouns, and adjectives

    The successful applicant **needs to be able to** travel a lot.
    It must **be great to be able to** speak several foreign languages.

- as a participle

    **Being able to** drive gives you much more freedom.

---

#### TIP

*Managed to do* and *succeeded in doing* are often used as alternatives to *was/ were able to*.
Rotherham **weren't able to / didn't manage to** hold on against Oxford.
We **were able to reach / succeeded in reaching** the summit on the third attempt.

---

# 75 Can and could (theoretical possibility)

## Can

A We use *can* to talk about theoretical possibility. This is not when we express the likelihood or probability of something, but when we state that it is possible for events and situations to happen. The most common uses of can in this way include:

- to say that events and situations are generally possible
  *You **can** get things much more cheaply online compared to in shops.*
  *Anyone **can** become 'famous for fifteen minutes' these days.*
  *Accidents **can** happen!*
  *We **can** say 'If I was' or 'If I were'.*
  ***Can** you book tickets in advance?*

- to talk about something that is possible on a particular occasion
  *I **can** wait for you in Reception.*
  *We **can** have the meeting on Thursday or Friday.*
  *We **can't** sit here – the table's reserved.*
  *But we **can** sit here if you like.*

- to talk about things that sometimes happen or to express characteristic behaviour
  *It **can** rain a lot in Rome in November.*

*The traffic **can** get very bad at rush hour.*
*Some snakes **can** grow up to ten metres.*
*Demonstrations **can** often end in violence.*
*Sarah **can** get quite jealous at times.*

• to express possible solutions to a problem or possible actions
   *We've got two options. We **can** go by bus or by train.*
   *What **can** we do to help? ~ Well, you **can** start by tidying the kitchen.*

### Could

B  We use *could* as the past tense of *can* when expressing possibility in the past.
   *Thomson was a great player, but he **could** get a bit complacent at times.*
   *Some dinosaurs **could** weigh up to 100 tonnes.*
   *Sorry I **couldn't** see you last night.*
   *You **could** get a loaf of bread for 10p when I was a child.*

C  We use *could* to make suggestions and to express possible solutions.
   *We **could** go by bus, but it takes about five hours.*
   *What can we do to help? ~ Well, you **could** start by tidying the kitchen.*
   *We **could** go for a walk later if it stops raining.*

We use *could always* to give emphasis to a possible solution. We also use *can always*.

*We **could always** go by bus, but it takes about five hours.*
*You don't like your job? You **can always** quit.*

D For *can/can't/could* to express probability or likelihood ▶ 78.

### Be able to

E We can sometimes use *be able to* instead of *can/could* to talk about possibility. However, this is usually in more formal contexts.

*Are you **able to** book at the restaurant?*

We use *be able to* in other tenses and forms.

*You've **never been able to** park here.*
*We **might be able to** book our tickets in advance.*

---

**TIP**

We can sometimes use *it is/was possible to* instead of *can*.
**It's possible** for anyone **to** become famous.
**It's possible to** go by bus or by train.
Not so long ago, **it was possible to** buy a car for a few hundred pounds.

We do not usually use *it's possible to* when expressing things that sometimes happen, or characteristic behaviour.
NOT *It's possible to rain a lot in Rome in November.*

---

# 76 *Can, could, may,* and *be able to* (permission and prohibition)

## Can

A We use *can* and *can't* to talk about what is permitted or prohibited according to official rules, regulations, and laws.

> Residents **can** use the hotel gym free of charge.
> **Can** we park here?
> You **can't** smoke in public buildings.

B We also use *can* and *can't* to talk about permission given by an individual.

> You **can** watch TV when you've done your homework.
> My boss says I **can't** take any more time off work this month.

We can also use *may*, but this is less common and is more formal.

> You **may** begin the test when you are ready.

## Could

C We use *could* as the past tense of *can* when expressing what was permitted or prohibited in the past.

> In the UK, women **couldn't** vote until 1918. Even then, only women over 30 **could** vote.

*Sorry I'm late. I **couldn't** leave work any earlier.*

## Be able to

D  We use *be able to* to express permission and prohibition when using perfect tenses.

*Women **have been able to** vote since 1925.*

E  We can also use *be able to* with other tenses and forms, such as *will* and *be going to*, infinitives, and participles. This is usually as a more formal alternative to *can*.

*Do you think you'**ll be able to** take next Friday off work?* (Do you think you can take …)
*We hope to **be able to** change our booking on the ferry.* (We hope we can change …)

## Asking for permission

F  We use *can*, *could*, or *may* to ask for permission to do something. *Could* is generally considered as more tentative or polite than *can*, and *may* is considered yet more polite and formal.

***Can** we use the photocopier?*
***Could** I take next Friday off work?*
***May** I be excused for a moment?*

G  We use phrases such as *may I ask*, *may I suggest*, *may I remind you*, etc. in formal contexts to precede what we say.

*May I ask* who else knows about this?
*May I remind you* that the previous
government created this situation?

We can also use *can* and *could* in a
similar way.
*Could I suggest* that we take a short
break here?

H  For *can*, *could*, and *may* for requests
   ▶ 77.

### Be allowed to

I  We can use the passive form *be allowed
   to* as an alternative to *can*, *could*, and
   *be able to* to emphasize that we are
   talking about a rule or prohibition.
   You're *not allowed to* smoke in here.
   *Are* you *allowed to* wear jeans at work?
   The best thing about this job is *being
   allowed to* choose my own hours.

J  The active form is also possible when
   you want to say who has made the rule.
   My parents *didn't allow me to* play
   computer games when I was younger.

---

**TIP**

We very often use *You can* or *You can't*
to talk about general rules or laws that
apply to everyone.
*You can't* park here.
*You can* vote when you're 18.
*Can you* take photos in the museum?

---

# 77 *Can, could, may, would,* and *will* (requests and offers)

## Requests with *can, could,* and *may*

A  We most commonly make requests with *can* or *could*. *Could* is generally considered more tentative, polite, or formal than *can*.

> **Can you** help me for a minute?
> **Could you** close the door, please?
> **Can I** borrow your pen?
> **Could I** open the window?

B  We can also use *may I/we*, which is often considered even more polite or formal. We do <u>not</u> use *may you*.

> **May I** sit here?
> NOT *May you help me?*

C  To ask to receive things we often use *can/could I have …?*

> **Can I have** your address?
> **Could I have** a receipt please?

## Phrases for requesting

D  We can use *would you mind …?* to make our requests more tentative, polite, or formal. Note the different patterns, according to whether we request the listener to do something or to allow something. Also note the use of the past subjunctive after *would you mind if I …?* ▶ 24.

> **Would you mind giving** this book
> to Jane?
> **Would you mind if I closed** the
> window?

E   We can also use *do you mind …?*
    This is slightly less tentative, polite, or
    formal than *would you mind …?*
> **Do you mind waiting** a few minutes?
> **Do you mind if I close** the window?

F   We can also use *is it OK if …?* to make
    informal requests.
> **Is it OK if** I use the phone?
> NOT *Is it OK using the phone?*

## Offers with *can* and *will/'ll*

G   We most commonly use *can* to
    make offers.
> **Can** we help you?
> **Can** I carry your bags for you?
> Peter **can** take you to the station.

H   We also use *will/'ll*.
> **I'll** help you.
> Peter **will** take you to the station.

    We do not use the full form *will* with
    pronouns when we make an offer.
> NOT *I will help you.*

I   We often use *can/'ll … if you like*.
> I **can** make the coffee **if you like**.
> **I'll** email Kara **if you like**.

## Phrases for offering

J   We can use *would you like (me to) …?*
    to make our offers more tentative,
    polite, or formal.
      **Would you like** a drink?
      **Would you like me to help** you?

K   We can also use *do you want (me to) …?*
    to make an offer. This is more neutral in
    tone than *would you like …?*
      **Do you want** something to drink?
      **Do you want me to cook** dinner?

    Note that we do <u>not</u> use a that-clause
    after *would you like …?* and *do you
    want …?*
      *Would you like me to come with you?*
      NOT *Would you like that I come
      with you?*

L   We can also use *let me …* to make an
    offer to do something ▶ 95.
      **Let me help** you with the washing up.

---

### TIP

To request things in a shop or restaurant
we can use *can/could I have …?*
(e.g. **Can I have** a sparkling water
please?). However, we often just say
the thing we want, adding *please*.
*A large cappuccino, please.*
*A pack of aspirin, please.*

When ordering food, we often use
*I'll have …*.
**I'll have** the risotto.

# 78 *Might, may, could, can,* and *must* (likelihood, probability, certainty)

A We use *might*, *may*, *could*, *can*, and *must* to express the likelihood, probability, or certainty of something.

## *Might* and *may* (future likelihood)

B We use *might* and *may* when we think that something is, or isn't, likely in the future. *Might* is generally more common than *may* in informal spoken English.

> It **might** rain later.
> I **might not** go to France next month after all.
> There **may** be a slight delay.
> We **may not** get there in time.

C We can also use *could*, but this is less common than *might* or *may* when talking about the future. We do <u>not</u> use *could not* in this way.

> It **could** rain later.
> Don't go now. Our bus **could** arrive soon.
> NOT *It couldn't rain later.*

D We do not use *can* or *can't* to express future likelihood.

> NOT *It can rain later.*
> NOT *Our bus can arrive soon.*

## *Might, may, could,* and *can* (present likelihood)

**E** We use *might, may,* and *could* when we think that something is, or isn't, likely in the present. This is often when we are making deductions based on present evidence.

> I think this **may** be our taxi.
> The supermarket **might** still be open.
> Elena **might not** be home yet.
> This **could** be Sam's bag.

We do <u>not</u> use *could not* in this way.
NOT ~~Elena could not be home yet.~~

**F** We use *can* only in questions.

> Who **can** that be at this time of night?
> NOT ~~The supermarket can still be open.~~

## *Must* and *can't* (certainty)

**G** We use *must* when we are certain about something. This is often when we deduce something.

> You haven't eaten all day. You **must** be hungry.
> My keys **must** be here somewhere.
> He **must** like spaghetti a lot. He eats so much of it!

**H** The opposite of this is *can't*. We use *can't* when we are certain something is not possible.

> You've just had a huge pizza – you **can't** still be hungry.

That **can't** be Kim's coat. It's too big.
This **can't** be right. There must be a
mistake.
NOT ~~You've just had a huge pizza —
you mustn't still be hungry.~~

We can also use *cannot* to emphasize
that we are shocked, surprised, or
disbelieving.
This **cannot** be true!

I   In UK English, we do not use *mustn't*
when we are certain something is not
possible.
NOT ~~You mustn't still be hungry.~~
However, this is sometimes possible in
American English.

### Have (got) to be

J   We can also use *have to be* or *have got
to be* as an alternative to *must* to talk
about something we are certain about.
This is more common in informal
contexts.
My wallet **has to be** here somewhere.
That **has got to be** the worst film I've
ever seen.
You**'ve got to be** joking!

### Past likelihood/certainty

K   We express likelihood and certainty in
the past with *must/might/may/could/
can't* + *have* + past participle.
Elena **might not have left** work yet.

Peter's not here yet. He **could've missed** his bus.
Anna wasn't at the meeting. She **must've forgotten** about it.
You **can't/couldn't have seen** Jack earlier this morning. He's in New York at the moment.

Note that *can't have* and *couldn't have* have the same meaning. Note that we do not use *can have* in this way.

L For *can/could* to express theoretical possibility ▶ 75.

---

**TIP**

There are a number of expressions and exclamations using *You must/can't be ...*.
*You must be joking!*
*You must be mad!*
*You can't be serious!*

---

# 79 *Will*

## Form

**A** The short form of *will* is *'ll*. In written English, we generally only use *'ll* after pronouns.

*I'll send you the itinerary tomorrow.*

In spoken English we often pronounce *will* as *'ll*.

*That'll be Dennis on the phone.*
*The taxi'll be here in a minute.*

**B** The negative of *will* is *won't*. But we can sometimes use *'ll not*.

*Jack **won't** be ready yet.*
*I **won't** have a coffee.*
OR *I'll **not** have a coffee.*

We can use *will not* in more formal contexts and for emphasis.

*He **will not** listen to a word I say!*

## Future meaning

**C** We use *will* in a number of ways to talk about the future ▶ 29,30.

*What time **will** you be leaving?*
*I'll be at work all day tomorrow.*
*Ministers **will** meet on Friday to discuss the matter.*
*There **will** possibly be snow in the north overnight.*
*I think you'll really enjoy the film.*

## Present and past supposition

**D** We use *will* to express a supposition or assumption or to draw conclusions about something in the present.

> *I'll get the phone – it'll be Dasha.*
> *Hurry up! The taxi **will** be waiting for us.*
> *The car **won't** start.*

We use *will* + perfect infinitive to make assumptions about something in the past.

> *Their wedding **will have cost** a fortune.*
> *I imagine Claire's plane **will have arrived** by now.*

## Typical behaviour

**E** We use *will* to talk about predictable, typical, or characteristic behaviour, such as habits.

> *I'll usually go for a run two or three times a week.*
> *Most evenings, we'll watch TV for an hour or so.*

Note that this use of *will* is similar to using the present simple to talk about habits, but we use *will* to emphasize that the behaviour is predictable or assumed, and not a 'fact'.

**F** We also use *will* to express annoyance or irritation. When we use it in this way we put the spoken stress on *will*.

> *He **will** keep playing that awful song.*

*My sister **will** insist on borrowing my clothes all the time.*

G We also use *will* to talk about the natural behaviour or properties of things.
*Many animal species **will** mate for life.*
*Chlorine **won't** react with oxygen.*

## Offers and requests

H We can use *will* as a formal way of offering or requesting something.
***Will** you have some more soup?*
***Will** you wait here for a moment?*

## Volition

I We use *will* to express volition. In other words, we use it to say that we are making free choices or decisions, or to show willingness.
*I'll have the chicken, please.*
*Can someone help me? ~ I **will**.*
*I'll lend you the money if you like.*

This use of *will* often refers to the future ▸ 29, 30.
*I'll phone you tomorrow.*

For *will* and *shall* ▸ 29.

---

### TIP

When we first discover that things don't function correctly, we use *won't start*, *won't work*, etc.
*The car **won't start**.*
*The kettle **won't turn off**.*
*The window **won't close** properly.*

# 80 *Would*

## Form

A The short form of *would* is *'d*. In written English, we generally use *'d* only after pronouns.

> *I'd love to come with you.*
> *She'd help if she could.*

In spoken English we often pronounce *would* as *'d*.

> *A weekend in Paris? That'd be great!*
> *I think the train'd be a better idea.*

B The negative of *would* is *wouldn't*. We can sometimes use *'d not*, but this is not common.

> *I wouldn't do that if I were you.*
> *I'd not do that if I were you.*
> *Sorry I'm late. The car wouldn't start.*

We use *would not* in more formal contexts and for emphasis.

> *I would not recommend your hotel to anyone.*
> *Would you eat here again? ~ I would not!*

## Hypothesis

C The main use of *would* is to express a hypothetical situation.

> *I'd love to be a professional photographer.*
> *What would you do in my situation?*
> *You wouldn't be much use in a crisis!*

**D** We often use *would* in conditional sentences ▶ 33–36 and after *if only* and *wish* ▶ 37.

*If I could, I'd take a year off work and go travelling.*
*If I were you, I'd look for a new job.*
*I wish it **would** stop raining.*

## Tentativeness

**E** We use *would* to make what we say more tentative, tactful, or polite.

*We'd prefer to meet a little sooner if possible.*
*It **would** seem that we disagree.*
*Extending the deadline **wouldn't** be possible, I'm afraid.*
***Would** you wait here for a moment?*
*There'll be a lot of disagreement I'd imagine.*

For more about this use of would ▶ 109.

The phrases *would like/mind/rather* for making requests and offers and when stating preferences are examples of this use of *would* ▶ 24, 77.

***Would** you **like** some more tea?*
*I **wouldn't mind** going out tonight actually.*
*I'd **rather** get a later flight if that's OK.*

## Past form of *will*

**F** We use *would* as the past form of *will*:

• in reported speech or thoughts ▶ 45–47

*Younis said he'd be late.*
*I knew Brazil **would** win.*

- for past typical behaviour or habits
  ▶ 20
  *I **would** often be at work until seven
  in the evening in my old job.*

- for the future in the past
  *Formed in Liverpool in the late
  1950s, the Beatles **would** eventually
  go on to become the most famous pop
  group of all time.*

- for negative volition or refusals in
  the past ▶ 79
  *The bank **wouldn't** lend me any
  more money.*
  *No one **would** help me.*
  *Sorry I'm late. The car **wouldn't**
  start.*

---

**TIP**

We use *I'd say* to give a tentative
opinion.
***I'd say** it's going to snow.*
***Would you say** it's a good idea?*

# 81 *Must* and *have (got) to*

## *Must* and *mustn't*

A We use *must* to express:

- obligation
  *You **must** carry an ID card at all times.*
  *Women lawyers **must** wear a black skirt and jacket.*

- strong necessity
  *We **must** win this game.*
  *I really **must** make a start with my assignment.*

- strong advice, suggestion, or recommendation
  *You **must** visit the Louvre if you have time.*

B The negative is *mustn't*.
  *We **mustn't** be late.*
  *You **mustn't** say anything to Jackie.*

We can use the full form *must not* in more formal contexts and for emphasis.
  *You **must not** feed the animals.*
  *The situation **must not** be allowed to deteriorate.*

## *Have to*

C *Have to* has very similar meaning to *must* and they are often interchangeable.

*You **have to** carry an ID card at all times.* (OR *You **must** carry ...*)
*We **have to** win this game.* (OR *We **must** win ...*)
*Why **do** we **have to** leave so early?* (OR *Why **must** we ... ?*)

D Because *have to* is not a modal verb, we can use it in a variety of tenses and forms.

*We'**ve had to** change the room for the meeting tomorrow.*
*Why **are** we **having to** leave so early?*
*The government **will have to** raise another £3 billion.*
***Did** you **have to** wear a uniform when you were at school?*

## Have got to

E *Have got to* is a common alternative to *have to* in more informal contexts, especially in speaking.

*We'**ve got to** win this game.*
*Why **have** we **got to** leave so early?*

However, we generally use *have to* for habitual or repeated obligation.

*I **have to** take my son to the gym club every Thursday.*

## Must or have (got) to?

F There is sometimes a difference between *must* and *have (got) to*. To express or emphasize that the obligation is imposed by someone else or by some other external pressure, such as a rule or law, we generally use *have (got) to*.

*I don't want to leave, but I **have to***.
*I**'ve got to** give a presentation at work.*

G For *must* and *have (got) to* to express possibility, likelihood, and certainty ▶ 78.

## Don't have to

H We use *don't have to* to say that someone is <u>not</u> obliged to do something.

*Sonia **doesn't have to** come with us.*
*We **don't have to** wear a tie at work.*

We do not use *mustn't* in this way.
NOT ~~Sonia mustn't come with us ....~~

## Past tense

I We use *had to* as the past tense of both *must* and *have to*.

*I **had to** go to Berlin for work last week.*
*The minister **had to** resign.*
*We **had to** wear a uniform at school.*

J We use *didn't have to* as the past tense of *don't have to*.

*We **didn't have to** go to school today.*

### TIP

We tend to use *must* (and not *have to*) in signs and notices even though we are expressing rules or laws.
*Seat belts **must** be worn.*
*Visitors **must** report to Reception.*

# 82 *Need* (necessity)

**A** We use *need* to say what is necessary or what is required. We can use *need* as both an ordinary verb and as a modal verb. It is therefore sometimes called a semi-modal verb.

**B** We use *need* as an ordinary verb in the following patterns:

- *need* + object

  I **need a drink**.
  Ben **needs a new coat**.
  Jim's OK. He **doesn't need any help**.
  **Do** you **need anything else**?

- *need* + to-infinitive

  I **need to make** a phone call.
  We **don't need to leave** just yet.
  Why **do** you **need to speak** to Abdul?
  Sorry I'm late. I **needed to stop** for petrol on the way.

  We also use *need* + object + to-infinitive

  I **need you to help** me.
  **Do** you **need someone to be** with you?

- *need* + -ing with passive meaning

  The grass **needs cutting**. (= The grass needs to be cut.)
  **Does** this shirt **need washing**?
  (= Does this shirt need to be washed?)

## 82

### Needn't and needn't have

C We can sometimes use *needn't* as an alternative to *don't/doesn't need to*. Here, *needn't* is a modal verb.

> We **needn't** leave until 5.30.
> OR We **don't need to** leave until 5.30.

D We can use *needn't have* + past participle as the past form, as an alternative to *didn't need to*.

> You **needn't have bought** me a present.
> OR You **didn't need to buy** me a present.

E We do not use *need* in the affirmative as a modal verb in this way.

> NOT ~~We need leave.~~

We can, however, sometimes use the modal form of *need* in questions.

> **Need** we do anything yet?

### Didn't need to and needn't have

F If someone does something that was not necessary, we can use either *didn't need to* or *needn't have*.

> I **needn't have worried**. Everything was fine in the end.
> OR I **didn't need to worry**. Everything was fine in the end.

However, if someone doesn't do something because they realize in

advance that it is not necessary, then
we must use *didn't need to*.

> I **didn't need to get up**, so I stayed in bed.
> NOT ~~I needn't have got up, so I stayed
> in bed.~~

## Need, must, and have (got) to

G We sometimes use *must* and *have (got)*
*to* to express necessity ▶ 81. *Must*, *have*
*(got) to*, and *need (to)* are therefore
sometimes interchangeable, with little
difference in meaning.

> We **need to** / **have got to** / **must** leave
> *after lunch*.
> **Do** we **need to** / **Do** we **have to** / **Must**
> we **book** in advance?

H *Don't/doesn't need to*, *needn't*,
and *don't/doesn't have to* are also
sometimes interchangeable.

> You **don't need to** / **needn't** / **don't**
> **have to** rush. We've got plenty of time.

---

**TIP**

*Do you need a hand (with) ...?* is a
common and useful question to ask if
someone needs help with something.
*Those bags look heavy.* **Do you need**
**a hand?**
**Do you need a hand with** *your bags?*
**Do you need a hand** *filling in the form?*

---

## 83 Should, ought to, had better, and be supposed to

### Should

A We use *should* in a number of ways.

- To say what we think is the correct or best thing to do. We often use it for advice and suggestions.

    *You really **should** stop smoking.*
    *You **shouldn't** eat so much pre-packaged fast food.*
    ***Should** I phone him?*

- To say what is correct or to make corrections.

    *You wrote '.com'. It **should** be '.co.uk'.*
    *It **shouldn't** be £52.50. It **should** be £42.50.*

- To say what we think is probable or what we expect to happen.

    *We **should** arrive at about 5.30.*
    *Lunch **should** be ready in ten minutes.*
    *Freddy **should** be leaving work now.*

    But we do <u>not</u> usually use *should* in this way for negative ideas when things don't go according to plan.

    *I'm afraid we'**ll be** about half an hour late.*
    NOT ~~I'm afraid we should be about half an hour late.~~

## Past tense of *shall*

B We use *should* as the past tense of *shall* in reported speech or thoughts ▶ 47.

*Dave was wondering what time we **should** meet.*

## Tentativeness

C We can sometimes use *should* to make what we say more tentative. However, this can sometimes sound quite formal and even old-fashioned.

*I **should** be delighted to speak at the conference.* (= I would be delighted …)

*If you **should** see Oliver, please pass on my best regards.* (= If you see Oliver …)

*I was amazed that anyone **should** do such a terrible thing.* (= … anyone would do such …)

*Take your umbrella in case it **should** rain.* (= … in case it rains.)

## *Ought to*

D We can use *ought to* as an alternative to *should* for advice and suggestions and to say what we expect to happen.

*You really **ought to** stop smoking.*

*New Zealand **ought to** beat Argentina.*

E It is possible to use *ought to* in negatives and questions, but we generally prefer to use *should*.

*You **oughtn't to** eat so much fast food.*

*You **shouldn't** eat so many sweets.*

## 83 Past form

F The past form is *should/ought to +
have* + past participle.
> We got lost. We **should've taken** a map.
> You **shouldn't have told** her! It was
> a secret.
> You really **ought to have spoken** to him.

### Had better and be supposed to

G *Had better* and *be supposed to* both
have similar meaning to *should*.

• We use *had better* to say what we think
is the correct or best thing to do.
> We**'d better** leave now or we'll be late.
> You**'d better not** spend everything
> at once.

• We use *be supposed to* to say
what is correct according to an
arrangement, rule, or general belief.
> You **were supposed to** be here an
> hour ago.
> You**'re not supposed to** park on
> double yellow lines.
> We**'re supposed to** eat five portions
> of fruit or vegetables each day.

---

**TIP**

We can use *must* for suggestions and
advice ▶ 81. It is generally stronger than
*should*.
> You **must** go to the Pantheon next time
> you're in Rome.
> We really **must** get together again soon.

---

# 84 Modal phrases and semi-modals

A There are a number of phrases which have similar meaning to modal verbs, and which we often use as alternatives to modal verbs. These phrases are called 'modal phrases'. One advantage of using modal phrases is that we can use them in many more tenses and patterns than modal verbs.

B We can express likelihood, probability, and certainty using a variety of words, phrases, and patterns as alternatives to the modal verbs *must*, *can't*, *might*, and *may* ▶ 78:

- *perhaps* and *maybe*
  **Perhaps** Sam's got lost.
  **Maybe** we'll go to Spain this year.

- *possibly, probably, definitely*
  It's **possibly** going to rain later.
  I'll **probably** stay at home this evening.
  The train **definitely** leaves at 11.00.

- *it's possible/probable/(un)likely (that)* …
  **It's possible** we'll be late.
  **It's probable that** the election will be held in May.
  **It's unlikely that** I'll be there.

- *be bound/certain/sure/(un)likely to …*
  It's **bound to** rain later.
  The cost **is likely to** be about €1000.

- *be certain/sure/positive (that) …*
  **Are** you **certain that** you can finish
  the report by Friday?
  **I'm sure** everything will be OK.
  He's **positive that** you'll like it.

### Be … to

C There are a number of phrases with the
pattern *be … to*.

- We use *be able to* as an alternative
  to *can/could* to express ability and
  possibility ▶ 74, 75.
  I **won't be able to** leave work before
  six, I'm afraid.
  I've **been able to** ski since I was
  about four.

- We use *be allowed/permitted to* as
  alternatives to *can/could/may* to
  express formal permission and
  prohibition ▶ 76.
  You're **not allowed to** take photos.
  Prisoners **are permitted to** have
  visitors once a week.

- We use *be supposed to* as an alternative
  to *should* to express what is correct,
  expected, or arranged ▶ 83.
  You're **not supposed to** park here.
  I'm **supposed to** be meeting Larry
  this evening.

## Semi-modals

D There are a number of semi-modal
verbs that have a similar meaning to
modal verbs.

• We use *have (got) to* with similar
meaning to *must* ▶ 81.
*I'm going to **have to** decline your
invitation I'm afraid.*
*You**'ve got to** be joking!*
*I don't want to go to school today! ~
You**'ve got to**.*

• We use *ought to* with similar
meaning to *should* ▶ 83.
*I really **ought to** be going soon.*

• We use *had better* with similar
meaning to *should* ▶ 83.
*The government **had better** start
listening to the voters.*
*When are we leaving? ~ Well,
we**'d better** get going in about five
minutes.*

### TIP

*Dare* can be an ordinary verb and
a modal verb. It can be used either
with or without *to*. The negative and
question forms can be with or without
the auxiliary verb *do*.
*Will anyone **dare** criticize the
government?*
*I'm surprised you **dare to** confront her!*
*I **didn't dare** say anything.*
*I **daren't** tell her.*

# 85 Overview of modal verbs

The main uses of the modal verbs are outlined below. For more detail and for other uses ▶ 73–84.

| Modal verb | Main uses | Example |
|---|---|---|
| can | • ability<br>• possibility<br>• permission<br>• deduction | *Erica **can** speak Polish.*<br>*We **can** get the bus home.*<br>*You **can't** park here.*<br>*This **can't** be correct.* |
| could | • past ability<br>• past possibility<br>• past permission<br>• deduction | *I **could** walk at nine months.*<br>*We **couldn't** get a ticket.*<br>*I **couldn't** leave work early.*<br>*This **could** be Jack's coat.* |
| must | • obligation<br>• necessity<br>• deduction<br>• advice/suggestion | *You **must** wear a suit.*<br>*We **must** leave in five minutes.*<br>*You **must** be John.*<br>*You **must** visit the Blue Mosque.* |

| | | |
|---|---|---|
| *might* | • likelihood | I ***might*** get a new phone. |
| | • deduction | This ***might*** be Jane's car. |
| *may* | • likelihood | There ***may*** be a delay. |
| | • deduction | I think this ***may*** be our taxi. |
| *should* | • what is correct | The green light ***should*** be on. |
| | • advice/suggestion | You ***should*** exercise more. |
| | • expectation | We ***should*** arrive soon. |
| *would* | • hypothesis | What ***would*** you do? |
| | • tentativeness | There ***would*** seem to be a problem. |
| | • past typical behaviour | We'***d*** never agree on anything. |
| *will* | • volition | I'***ll*** help you. |
| | • prediction/assumption | You'***ll*** love the exhibition. |
| | • supposition | That'***ll*** be Alex at the door. |
| | • habit | We'***ll*** watch TV most evenings. |
| *shall* | • suggestion | ***Shall*** we meet at 7.30? |

# 86 *Be*

For the form of *be* ▶ 9, 14.

**A** We use *be* as an auxiliary verb in:

- continuous tenses ▶ 11, 17–19
  *It's raining.*
  *Where **are** you going?*
  *Have you **been** waiting long?*

- passive forms ▶ 39
  *The website **is** updated every day.*
  *Where **was** the first World Cup held?*
  *My room **hasn't been** cleaned.*

**B** We use *be* as a main verb to link a subject with its complement (what describes, defines, or relates to the subject). *Be* is sometimes referred to as a 'linking verb', or 'complement verb' ▶ 1. Uses of *be* in this way include:

- identity and definition
  *Jim and Alice **are** my neighbours.*
  *Anna's my cousin.*
  *A flute **is** a musical instrument.*

- nationality and origin
  *They're not French. He's Canadian and she's from Belgium.*

- someone's job
  *I'm a teacher.*
  *My mum **was** a lawyer.*

- age
  *I'm* 18.
  *It's* about 400 years old.

- personality, character, feelings, and behaviour
  *She's* friendly.
  *I was* tired this morning.
  *Are* you OK?

- properties and qualities
  *The exam was* easy.
  *She's* very tall.
  *The apps market is* very competitive.

- possession
  *This is* our car.
  *Are* these your sunglasses?

- time, days, and dates
  *The bus was* late.
  *It's* 6.30.
  *It was* a Thursday. *It was* May 5th.

- weather and temperature
  *It's* sunny.
  *It isn't* cold.

- prices and cost
  *The trousers are* €50.
  *How much is* the bill?

Note that we sometimes use *be* where a different verb is used in other languages. For example:
  *She's* 22. NOT ~~She has 22.~~
  *I'm* cold. NOT ~~I have cold.~~

C  We use the continuous form of *be* (*is being*, *were being*, etc.) to talk about temporary behaviour or states.
   *The weather **is being** a bit unpredictable these days.*
   *The children **are being** a bit noisy.*

D  We use *be* to talk about place and location.
   *Your keys **are** on the table.*
   *She's not here. She's in Milan.*
   *Where **were** you last night?*
   *I've just **been** in a meeting.*

E  We use *there + be* (*there is*, *there aren't*, *there were*, etc.) to say that something exists or doesn't exist.
   *There's a train at 3.30.*
   *There are billions of stars in the galaxy.*
   *Were there any tickets left?*
   *There hasn't been much rain recently.*

---

**TIP**

We can use *been* (the past participle of *be*) in the sense 'having gone somewhere and then left'. We use *gone* (the past participle of *go*) in the sense 'having gone somewhere and still being there'.
Compare the following sentences.
*Kara's been to the supermarket.*
(She went to the supermarket and then returned home.)
*Kara's gone to the supermarket.* (She is still at the supermarket.)

# 87 *Have*

**A** We use *have* as an auxiliary verb to form perfect tenses ▶ 15, 17, 19.
   ***Have*** *you seen my keys?*
   *It**'s** been raining all day.*
   *Sam might **have** gone out.*

**B** We use *have (got) to* as a semi-modal verb to express necessity and obligation ▶ 81 and to express certainty ▶ 78.
   *What time **do** we **have to** be at the airport?*
   *You**'ve got to** be joking!*

**C** We use *have got* + noun to talk about possession or characteristics ▶ 88.
   *I**'ve got** two brothers.*
   *Jane**'s got** long hair.*

**D** We use *have* + someone/something + active participle to mean 'cause something to happen'.
   *Mum **had us tidying** our rooms all morning.*
   *Dick's so funny. He **had us** all **crying** with laughter.*

We can also use *have* + someone/something + infinitive without *to* when we arrange for someone to do something for us.
   *We**'re having somebody cut down** the old apple tree.*

241

For *have/get something done* ▸ 40.

E We use *have* + noun to talk about certain actions and experiences. These include:

- meals: *have breakfast/dinner*, etc.
  *We're **having** a late lunch today.*

- food and drink: *have a drink / a burger / a coffee / a pizza*, etc.
  *I'll **have** a coffee and a croissant please.*

- everyday activities: *have a shower / a rest / a walk / a nap*, etc.
  *She always **has** a little nap after lunch.*

- events: *have a lesson / a meeting / a party / a chat / a holiday*, etc.
  *Suki's **having** a party next Friday.*

- positive experiences: *have fun / a good time / a good day / a laugh*, etc.
  ***Did** you **have** a good time?*

- negative experiences: *have a bad day / a problem / an argument / an accident*, etc.
  *Alex **had** an accident on his bike this morning. He's fine now, though.*

F We use the imperative form of *have* when we wish people a good or enjoyable time.
  ***Have** a nice day!*
  ***Have** fun!*
  ***Have** a good trip!*

G We can sometimes use *have a* + noun instead of using a verb, for example: *have a go* (= experience or try something), *have a look, have a taste, have a guess.*

> I **had a go** on Billy's new motorbike this morning.
> I can't open the window. Will you **have a go**?
> There's a problem with my computer. Can you **have a look** at it?

H We use *have* + noun to offer something.

> Please, **have** a seat.
> **Have** some more cake.

### TIP

In your language you may use a different verb where English uses *have*, or you may use *have* where English uses a different verb. For example, in English we do not say ~~I have twenty years old.~~ Try to notice where the use of *have* in English and your language is the same or different.

# ∞ 88 *Have got*

**A** *Have got* has a number of meanings and uses. Here are some of the most common.

**B** We use *have got* + object to talk about possessions and things we own.
> **I've got a new mobile**.
> **Have you got your own office** at work?

We can use *have got ... on/with me*, etc. to say that we have something in our possession at the moment.
> **I haven't got** any money **on me**.
> **Have you got** your laptop **with you**?

**C** We use *have got* to talk about things being available. We often use *have got* in this way in places such as shops and restaurants.
> **Have you got** this dress in a size ten?
> **They've got** lots of vegetarian dishes.

**D** We use *have got* to talk about the features, characteristics, or qualities of someone or something.
> **Sam's got** short fair hair.
> **Has** the school **got** a swimming pool?
> **You'd got** a beard last time I saw you.

**E** We use *have got* to talk about family and other relationships.
> **I've got** two brothers.

*Have* Lucy and Steve **got** any children?
**Has** Darren **got** a girlfriend?

F   We use *have got* to talk about illness
and other medical conditions.
*I've got* a headache.
*He's got* a heart condition.

G   We can sometimes use *have* as an
alternative to *have got*. This is more
common in questions and negatives
and when talking about the past.
*Do* you **have** your own office?
*You* **had** a beard last time I saw you.

We can also use *have* in the affirmative,
but this can sound more formal.
*I* **have** an aunt who lives in New York.
*The company* **has** two subsidiaries.

H   We use *have got to* as a semi-modal
verb to express necessity/obligation
▶ 81 and certainty/deduction ▶ 78.
*What time* **have** we **got to** be at the
airport?
*My keys* **have got to** be here
somewhere.

---

### TIP

*I haven't (got) a clue* and *I've (got) no
idea* are useful expressions for saying
we don't know something.
*Where's Oliver? ~ **I've no idea**.
*What's his name? ~ **I haven't got a clue**.

# 89 *Do*

**A** We use *do* as an auxiliary verb in a simple tense to form the negative, to form questions and short answers, and to add emphasis ▶ 3,4,8,13.

*I **don't** drink coffee.*
***Do** you live here? ~ Yes, I **do**.*
*Jackie **does** look like her sister.*

**B** *Do* as a main verb has the general meaning of 'perform an activity'.

- We use *do* when we do not specify the activity, for example in questions and negatives.

  ***Are** you **doing** anything tonight?*
  *What **did** you **do** at the weekend?*
  *He **didn't do** anything wrong.*

- *What do you do?* etc. is a common question meaning 'What's your job?' etc.

  ***What do you do?*** *~ I'm a teacher.*
  ***What does he do?*** *~ He's a doctor.*

- There are many expressions in which we use *do* + noun phrase.

  *I'm **doing** a computer **course**.*
  *Can you **do** me **a favour**?*

For more expressions with *do* ▶ page 346.

- We use *do* + *the/some* + gerund for household activities. These include:

246

*cooking, cleaning, gardening, ironing, shopping, washing, washing up.*
  I need to **do some washing**.
  **Have** you **done the shopping**?

- We use *do* with some sports.
  These include: *athletics, gymnastics, judo/karate, yoga, a bungee jump, a marathon.*
    **Have** you ever **done yoga**?
    I'd never **do a bungee jump**!

- We use *do* + a speed to talk about how fast a vehicle travels.
    *A Formula One car can **do 300 kph**.*

C  We use *to do with* with *nothing* or *something* to mean 'be involved/connected with' or 'be responsible for'.
    *This mess has **nothing to do with me**.*
    *The problem is **something to do with** your anti-virus software.*

D  *Will do* can mean 'be enough'.
    *A sandwich **will do** – I'm not hungry.*
    ***Will** €10 **do** as a tip?*

### TIP

*How do you do?* is a formal but common greeting when we meet someone for the first time. Its meaning is similar to 'Hello, pleased to meet you.'
A: I'm James. **How do you do?**
B: **How do you do?**

Note the response is also *How do you do?*

# 90 *Make*

*Make* has a number of meanings and uses. Here are some of the most common.

**A** We use *make* to mean 'construct' or 'create'.
> They **make** the Mini in Oxford.
> **Did** you **make** this doll's house?

It can also be used to mean produce or prepare something.
> I **made dinner** last night.
> I'm going to **make a coffee**.
> Who **made this mess**?

We can also use *make* + someone + noun ▶ 2.
> My daughter **made me a new dress**.

**B** We use *make* + noun phrase to mean 'perform an action'.
> I need to **make a phone call**.
> Don't **make promises** you can't keep.
> Stop **making a fuss**!
> Who's **making that noise**?

For expressions with *make* ▶ page 346.

**C** We use *make* (*it to*) to mean 'attend'.
> Did you **make it to** the meeting?
> I won't **make** the lecture this afternoon.

**D** We use *make* to mean 'be in time for something'. We also use *make it* (*to* somewhere) in the same sense.

*If we hurry, we'll **make** the 10.15 bus.*
*Do you think we'll **make it to** the station in time?*
*He only just **made it**!*

**E** We also use *make it* to mean 'achieve success'.

*Chloe's got the talent to **make it** to the top.*

**F** We use *make* + adjective + noun to mean 'have the necessary qualities'.

*Do you think he'll **make a good prime minister**?*
*Julia and Danny **make a lovely couple**, don't they?*

**G** We use *be made from/of* + material to mean 'formed, produced, or manufactured from'.

*Glass **is made from** sand.*
*The sculpture **is made of** ice.*

Note that we generally use 'from' if the raw material is altered in the process and 'of' if it is not.

**H** We use *make* + someone/something + infinitive without *to* to mean 'cause someone to feel or do something' or 'cause something to happen'.

*Peeling onions always **makes me cry**.*
*The TV programme **made me angry**.*

We can also use *make* + someone/
something + adjective/noun.
*Too much chocolate **makes you fat**.*
*The books **make the box too heavy**.*

I We use *make* + someone + infinitive
without *to* to mean 'force someone to
do something'.
*They **made us wait** outside in the rain.*
*Mum **made me go to bed** early.*

Note that when we use the passive, we
use the to-infinitive.
*I **was made to go to bed** early.*

J There are a number of other useful
expressions with *make*. For example:
*Many people have to **make do** with
very little money.* (= manage/cope)
*Can you **make your way** to the exits?*
(= move towards)
*Let's **make a start**.* (= begin)

---

**TIP**

In your language you may use a
different verb where English uses *make*,
or you may use *make* where English
uses a different verb. For example, in
English we say **make** *a decision*, but
some other languages use a different
verb. Notice where the use of *make*
in English and in your language is the
same or different.

---

# 91 *Get*

*Get* has a number of meanings and uses.
Here are some of the most common.

A   We use *get* + noun phrase to mean
'obtain' or 'receive'.
   *I **got a new laptop** for my birthday.*
   *Did you **get Line's email address**?*
   *I **got 85%** in my English test.*

   We often use *get* to talk about things
   we buy, about earning money, and
   about illnesses.
   *I'm going to the shop **to get some bread**.*
   *I **got £10** for cleaning my dad's car.*
   *We all **got food poisoning** on holiday.*

B   We also use *get* + noun phrase to mean
'bring' or 'fetch'.
   *Can you **get my glasses** from the
   kitchen table?*
   *I'm just going to **get Lauren's coat**
   from the car.*

   We often use *get* in this way with an
   indirect object ▶ 2.
   *Could you get **me** a glass of water?*

C   We use *get* + indirect object + noun
phrase to mean 'buy or obtain
something for someone'. It can also
have the meaning 'give' when we obtain
something for someone as a gift.
   *I **got Dave a shirt** in the sales.*

*Tina **got me a book** for my birthday.*
***What did** Sue **get you** for Christmas?*
We can also use *get* + *for* ▶ 2.
*I **got a shirt for Dave** in the sales.*

D We use *get* + adjective to mean
'become something' or to talk about
things changing.
*We **got wet** when it rained.*
*It's **getting late**.*
*Are you **getting ready**?*
*Isn't Jimmy **getting tall**?*

There are also a number of useful
expressions using *get* + past
participle with the meaning 'become
something'. These include *get dressed*,
*get lost*, *get married*, and *get stuck*.
*Sorry we're late. We **got lost**.*
*We **got married** in 2008.*

E We use *get* + adverbial to mean 'travel
or arrive somewhere'.
*How do you **get to school**?*
*We **got home** at about midnight.*
*Call me when you **get to the hotel**.*

We also use *get* to talk about how we
travel.
*Let's **get a taxi**.*
*We **got the 10.30 bus**.*

**F** We use *get* + gerund to mean 'start or do something'.

> *Let's **get going** or we'll be late.*
> *OK, I'll **get cooking**, shall I?*

We also use the expressions *get on with* and *get round to* + gerund or noun phrase to mean '(finally) start to do something'.

> *Can you **get on with** the cooking?*
> *I'm sure he'll **get round to fixing** the light one day.*

**G** We use *get* + person/thing + active participle to mean 'cause someone to do something' or 'cause something to happen'. There is a focus on the activity in progress.

> *Some good old disco music **will get everyone dancing**.*
> *This new valve should **get it working**.*

We also use *get* + person/thing + to-infinitive. The focus is on the activity as a whole.

> *Can you **get Alex to tidy** his room?*
> *I can't **get the coffee machine to work**.*

**H** We use *get* + someone + to-infinitive when we arrange for somebody to do something for us.

> ***Who did** you **get to feed** the cats while you're away?*
> *We're **getting Jim's sister to design** the wedding dress.*

## 91

For *get* with the passive and for
*have/get something done* ▶ 40.

I   We use *get* + noun or question word to
mean 'understand something'.
*I **don't get it**!*
***Do** you **get what** I mean?*

J   We use *get* + to-infinitive to mean
'have the opportunity to do something'
or 'succeed in doing something' or
'manage to do something'.
*We **got to meet** the band after the gig!*
***Did** you **get to go** on Jim's motorbike?*
*We **didn't get to see** the film
unfortunately.*

---

**TIP**

Phrases with *get* are generally used
in more informal contexts such as
conversation and informal writing.
Compare the following:
*We'**ll get to** the hotel at about 6.30.*
(informal)
*We **shall arrive** at the hotel at
approximately 6.30.*
***Did** you **get to speak** to Yuko?* (informal)
***Did** you **manage to speak** to Yuko?*

---

# 92 *Go*

*Go* has a number of meanings and uses. Here are some of the most common.

A We use *go* + adverbial/preposition to mean 'move or travel somewhere'.
> *I'm going to London tomorrow.*
> *We went to a great little café last night.*
> *It's getting cold. Shall we go inside?*

There are many common and useful expressions that use *go* with this meaning. These include: *go to bed, go on holiday, go home, go out, go to university, go to work.*
> *I'm going to bed. Good night.*
> *It's time for us to go home.*
> *Where are you going on holiday?*
> *Where's Jack? ~ He's gone out.*

Note that we generally use *come* when the speaker or listener is or will be at the destination.
> *I'm not coming here again!*
> *Can you come and help me please?*

B *Go* on its own means 'leave'.
> *I'm going. See you later.*
> *Where's Julia? ~ I think she's gone.*

C We use *go* + gerund for leisure activities and shopping. These include: *camping, diving, fishing, shopping,* skating, skiing, snowboarding, surfing, swimming, walking.

*Let's **go swimming**.*
*I **went shopping** this morning.*
*We**'re going surfing** at the weekend.*

D We use *go and* + infinitive without *to* to talk about going somewhere in order to do something ▶ 50.

*I**'ll go and see** when the bus leaves.*
*Let's **go and buy** some lunch.*
*I'm going to **go and get** the car tyres checked.*

We can also use *go* + to-infinitive to express purpose or the reason for going somewhere ▶ 56.

*I**'m going to get** some milk.*
*Lupi**'s gone to collect** the children.*

We also use *go for* + noun to express purpose.

*I**'m going for** a shower.*
*Gerta's **gone** to the shop **for** some more bread.*

E We use *go* with some adjectives in a few expressions to mean 'become something' or to explain how someone or something is behaving.

*He**'s gone mad**!*
*Is Max OK? He**'s gone a bit quiet**.*

**F**  We use *go* (*at*) to express the speed at
which something travels.
   *The new high-speed trains **go at** over
   200 kilometres per hour.*
   *How fast can your motorbike **go**?*

**G**  We use *go* + adverbial to give an
assessment of success or progress or to
talk about the state of something.
   *I think the interview **went well**.*
   *The lesson **went really slowly**.*
   *The office relocation **is going fine**.*

   *How did ... go?* and *how's ... going?* are
   common questions.
   ***How did** your exam **go**? ~ It went OK,
   I think.*
   ***How's** the course **going**? ~ It's really
   interesting, actually.*

   We use *how's it going?* to ask about life
   in general.
   ***How's it going**? ~ Fine thanks. And you?*

---

**TIP**

*Go wrong* and *go right* are useful
expressions for when a mistake is made
or when things do not go according
to plan.
*If you **go wrong**, start again.*
*Today was a disaster. Nothing **went right**.*

---

# 93 *Take*

*Take* has a number of meanings and uses. Here are some of the most common.

A  We use *take* + noun phrase (+ adverbial) in the general sense 'move or transport'. This could be:

- remove something from a place
  *Has anyone **taken my keys**?*
  *Sorry, I **took the last biscuit**.*

- transport or carry something or someone with you or accompany someone
  *Who's **taking Val to the station**?*
  *Can you **take these reports to Andrew**?*

We can also sometimes use two objects after *take* ▸ 2.
  *Can you **take Andrew these reports**?*

We can use *take* + someone + gerund for some leisure activities.
  *I **took the children swimming** this morning.*

Note that we use *bring* when the speaker or listener is or will be at the destination.
  *Don't forget to **bring your homework** to school tomorrow.*

B  We use *take* + noun phrase to mean 'reach for and hold something'.
   *Can you **take these books** for a moment?*
   *George **took his mother's hand**.*

C  We use *take* + time expression to talk about the duration of a journey or an action.
   *The bus **takes five minutes**.*
   ***How long does** the journey **take**?*

   We commonly use the expression *it* + *take* + time expression (+ to-infinitive).
   ***It took** us **two days**.*
   ***It takes an hour to get** to work.*
   ***How long does it take to get** to Oxford?*

   Note that for events such as films, appointments, and lessons we use *last*.
   *The lesson **lasts** 45 minutes.*

D  We use *it* + *take* + noun phrase + to-infinitive to say how many or much of something is needed.
   ***It took four people to move** the wardrobe.*
   ***It takes a lot of skill to make** the perfect soufflé.*

E  We use *take* + noun phrase to mean 'accept or receive something'.
   *Are you going to **take the job**?*
   *All the employees **took a 5% pay cut**.*

We use *take* + noun phrase to talk about being subjected to something.

> The houses **took a lot of damage** in the storm.
>
> The team **took a serious beating** by Arsenal and the final score was 4–0.

**F** We use expressions with *take* + noun phrase for certain actions:

- transport: *take the bus / the train / the metro / a taxi*, etc.

- food and medicine: *take milk / sugar / drugs / an aspirin*, etc.

- exams: *take an exam / a test*

- control: *take control / power / the lead / responsibility / office*

Other phrases include: *take advice / a break / a nap / (no) notice / offence / part / place / a photo / pity / a seat / sides / (your, etc.) time / a walk*

> Did you **take** many **photos** on holiday?
>
> **Take your time.** There's no rush.
>
> **Take no notice** – he's not being serious.

---

**TIP**

*Take ... for example* and *I take your point (about)* are two useful expressions for discussion and giving opinions.

A good England football team? **Take 1966 for example**.

OK, **I take your point about 1966**, but I don't agree about any other time.

---

# 94 *See*

*See* has a number of meanings and uses.
Here are some of the most common.

A We use *see* to talk about what is visible.
   *You can **see** for miles from the top floor.*
   *I **saw** you in the supermarket earlier.*
   *I can't **see** anything without my glasses.*

   We generally use *can('t) see* to talk
   about what it is or isn't possible to see
   at a particular moment.
   ***Can** you **see** Peter?*
   *I **can't see** Roger's car. Can you?*

B We use *see* + object to talk about more
   prolonged or deliberate activities. The
   meaning is similar to 'watch'.
   *We **saw the new Bond film** last night.*
   ***Did** you **see the fireworks display**?*

C We use *see* + object to mean 'meet' or
   'spend time with someone'.
   *I'm **seeing Alison** this evening.*
   *You should **see the doctor**.*
   *What do you want to **see me** about?*

D We use *see* + (that-)clause to talk about
   things we realize or learn.
   *I **see that Luke got promoted**.*

   We can also use *see* on its own.
   *This parking space is for residents
   only. ~ Oh, I **see**.*

**E** We use *see* + wh-clause or noun to mean 'understand'.

> *Do you see what I mean?*
> *Why are we setting off so early? I don't see the point.*

**F** We use *see* + wh-clause or if-clause to express an intention to investigate, discover, or find out something.

> *I'll see what time the film starts.*
> *Can you see if Jack's arrived yet?*

**G** We use *see to* + object to say that we take responsibility for doing something.

> *I'll see to the dinner tonight.*
> *Don't worry about booking the tickets. I'll see to it.*

---

### TIP

There are a number of useful expressions using *see*. These include:
*(I'll) see you later, as I see it, we'll see, you'll see.*
*I must be going now. **See you later.*** (used to say goodbye)
***As I see it**, it's a great idea.* (used to express an opinion)
*Can we go for a pizza later?* ~ ***We'll see**.* (used to say we will decide later)
*Everything will be OK. **You'll see**.* (used to say that the speaker will be proved correct)

# 95 *Let*

*Let* has a number of meanings and uses. Here are some of the most common.

A   We use *let's* (*not*) + infinitive without *to* to express a suggestion or an instruction to a group that includes the speaker.

*Let's **go** for a coffee.*
*Let's **have** a party.*
*Let's **not waste** any more time.*
*Let's **not be** late.*

We can use the full form *let us* (*not*) in more formal contexts and to add emphasis.

*Let us look in more detail at the results.*
*Let us not forget the lessons of the past fifty years.*

We can sometimes use *don't let's* as the negative, but this is uncommon.

*Don't let's make the same mistake again.*

B   We use the question tag *shall we?* with both *let's* and *let's not*.

*Let's get a taxi, **shall we?***
*Let's get down to business, **shall we?***
*Let's not be late again, **shall we?***

**C** We use *let's see* and *let's think* to show
we are thinking about or considering
something.

*What shall we have for dinner? ~*
***Let's see.** Why don't we have risotto?*
*What's the best way to get to Jim's
house? ~ **Let's think.** Yeah, I'd say get
the bus to the university and then walk.*

We can also use *let me see* and *let me
think* in the same way.

***Let me see.** Why don't we have risotto?*
***Let me think.** Yeah, I'd say get the bus
to the university and then walk.*

We also use *let's see* to say we should
wait to see how a situation develops,
often before making a decision.

*Can we go to the beach for my birthday
party? ~ **Let's see.***

**D** We use *let* + someone + infinitive
without *to* when we offer to help.

***Let me help** you.*
***Let us take** you to the station.*

We also use this pattern when we are
making a request.

***Let me have** a look at your new phone.*
***Let us hear** your news, then.*

In informal contexts, especially in speaking, we can use *let's* instead of *let me* when we are making a request.

**Let's** have a look at your new phone.
**Let's** see the photo.

E We use *let ... know* to mean 'tell or inform someone'.

Can you **let Sara know** about the party?

F We use *let* + object + infinitive without *to* as a more informal way of saying 'allow' ▶ 49.

My parents never **let me stay** up late during the week.
Do you think your boss will **let you leave** early on Friday?
You're hurting me! **Let me go**!

We also use *let* + object + adverbial.

The police **aren't letting the traffic through**.
Who **let the dogs out**?

---

### TIP

We can use *let's* or *let's not* as a response to a suggestion.
Shall we go to the beach? ~ Yeah, **let's**.
Why don't we eat out tonight? ~ **Let's not**. I'm a bit tired.

## 96 *Suggest* and *recommend*

We can use *suggest* and *recommend* in a number of patterns.

A   We use *suggest/recommend* + noun.
   *Claire **suggested Café Bleu** for lunch.*
   *I **recommend the pasta**.*

B   We use *suggest/recommend* + finite clause (with or without *that*).
   *I **suggest we wait here for a few minutes**.*
   *Are you **suggesting that we start again**?*
   *They **recommend that you book in advance**.*

   Note that when we report a current suggestion or recommendation using the past tense of *suggest* or *recommend*, we can generally use either the present or past tense of the following verb.
   *Thomas **suggested** that we **met/meet** at his house.*
   *My friend **recommended** we **didn't/ don't eat** here.*

   For tense changes when reporting ▶ 47.

C   We can also use *suggest/recommend* + gerund.
   *I **suggest waiting** here for a few minutes.*

*I **suggest not saying** anything just yet.*
*Alex **recommended staying** in York.*
*They **recommend booking** in advance.*

We do not use *suggest/recommend* +
to-infinitive.
NOT *I suggest to wait here.*
NOT *Alex recommended to stay in York.*

D We sometimes use *suggest/recommend*
with the present subjunctive. However,
today this is quite uncommon and can
sound a little old-fashioned ▶ 23.
*I **suggested** that she **leave** immediately.*
*We strongly **recommend** that Sarah*
***attend** the meeting.*

E We can use *recommend* + object +
to-infinitive. However, this can often
sound a little formal.
*They **recommend us to book** in*
*advance.*
*Simon **recommended us to visit** the*
*Musée d'Orsay.*

We do not use *suggest* in this way.
NOT *They suggested us to book in*
*advance.*

---

**TIP**

*What do you suggest?* and *What do you*
*recommend?* are useful questions.
*Taxi or bus? **What do you suggest?***
*The menu looks interesting. **What do***
***you recommend?***

# 97 *Prefer* and *would rather*

We use both *prefer* and *would rather* to talk about preferences. We can use them in a number of patterns.

## *Prefer*

A  We use *prefer* to talk about general preferences.

- We can use *prefer* + noun.
  *I don't drink much coffee. I **prefer tea**.*
  *Football's OK, but I much **prefer rugby**.*

- We can use *prefer* + gerund.
  *I don't ski. I **prefer snowboarding**.*

- We can also use *prefer* + to-infinitive, but this is less common.
  *I never read. I **prefer to watch** films.*

To mention an alternative we use *to*.
*I **prefer** coffee **to** tea.*
*I **prefer** snowboarding **to** skiing.*

We do not use the to-infinitive when we mention alternatives.
NOT *I prefer to watch films to to read.*

## *Would prefer*

B  We use *would prefer* + to-infinitive or noun for a particular situation or when we are talking hypothetically.
*I'd **prefer to go** by train.*
*Peas or beans? ~ I'd **prefer peas**.*

We do not use the gerund after *would prefer*.
>  NOT *I'd prefer going by train.*

To mention an alternative we use *rather than*.
>  *I'd prefer to go by train **rather than** by bus.*

After *rather than*, we can use the gerund or an infinitive without *to*.
>  *I'd prefer to stay here tonight **rather than drive/driving** home at this time.*

### Would rather

C  We use *would rather* + infinitive without *to* with similar meaning to *would prefer*.
>  *I'd **rather go** by train.*
>  *The government **would rather delay** the election for six months.*

To mention an alternative we use *than*.
>  *I'd **rather** go by train **than** by bus.*

We do not generally use *would rather* + noun.
>  *Tea or coffee? ~ I'd prefer coffee.*
>  NOT *I'd rather coffee.*

D  We use (*would*) *prefer/rather* + *not* for negative sentences.
>  *I **prefer not** to drive in the city.*
>  *I'd **prefer not** to go by bus.*
>  *I'd **rather not** have a starter if that's OK.*

We do not generally use *prefer* + *not* + gerund.

NOT ~~Most people prefer not driving in the city.~~

E   We can use *would prefer/rather* + finite clause. When we use this pattern with present or future meaning, we usually use the past subjunctive ▶ 24.

*They'd prefer we met at John's house.*
*They'd rather we arrived a bit earlier.*
*I'd rather you didn't smoke.*
*I'd prefer that you didn't do that.*

A present tense is possible, but less common. It makes things sound a little more immediate or direct.

*They'd rather we arrive a bit earlier.*
*I'd rather you don't smoke.*

To talk about a past action we can use *would rather* + someone + past perfect. This is usually when we are expressing regret or dissatisfaction.

*I'd rather you hadn't done that!*

---

**TIP**

We often use phrases such as *if that's ok*, *if possible*, and *if you don't mind* at the end of the sentence when stating preferences.
*I'd prefer tea if that's ok.*
*I'd rather leave now if possible.*
*I'd rather stay here if you don't mind.*

---

# 98 Introduction to multi-part verbs

**A** A multi-part verb consists of a verb and one or more particles.

*Can you **turn** the light **off**?*
*I **grew up** in Sheffield.*
*We've **run out of** time.*

Particles are words that we use as prepositions (e.g. *at*, *for*, *into*) or adverbs (e.g. *away*, *back*) in other contexts. Note that we can use many particles as both prepositions and adverbs (e.g. *across*, *in*, *off*, *on*, *out*, *up*).

There are three types of multi-part verb: phrasal verbs, prepositional verbs, and phrasal-prepositional verbs.

## Phrasal verbs

**B** A phrasal verb consists of a verb + adverb particle. There are many phrasal verbs in English. The meaning of the phrasal verb is often very different from the meaning of the verb and the adverb particle taken separately.

*What time shall we **set off**?* (= leave)
*They've **put** the meeting **off** until next week.* (= postponed)
*When's the new James Bond film **coming out**?* (being released)

For more on phrasal verbs ▶ 99, 100.

## Prepositional verbs

C A prepositional verb consists of a
verb + preposition. There are two main
types of prepositional verb.

- Some prepositional verbs are
similar to phrasal verbs in that the
meaning can be very different from
the meaning of the verb and the
preposition taken separately.
  *I **ran into** Elena in town this morning.*
  (= met by chance)
  *Can you **look after** Lauren this
  evening?* (= be responsible for)

  Note that this kind of prepositional
  verb is considered as a phrasal verb
  by some books and teachers.

  For more on this kind of
  prepositional verb ▶ 101.

- In the other kind of prepositional
verb, the verb and preposition are
used in their normal senses. The
meaning is usually clear from the
verb + preposition combination.
  *The solar system **consists of** the sun
  and its planets.*
  *Which team did Pele **play for**?*

  For more on this kind of
  prepositional verb ▶ 102.

# Phrasal-prepositional verbs

**D** A phrasal-prepositional verb consists of a verb + adverb particle + preposition. As with phrasal verbs and some prepositional verbs, the meaning is often very different from the meaning of the verb and the particles taken separately. Phrasal-prepositional verbs are sometimes known as three-part verbs.

>   Do you **get on with** your neighbours?
>   The printer's **run out of** ink.

For more on phrasal-prepositional verbs ▶ 103.

---

### TIP

When you see or hear a multi-part verb, notice if it has an object or not and in what position the object is. This will help you to determine what kind of multi-part verb it is and will help you to use it correctly.

## 99 Phrasal verbs (1)

A A phrasal verb is a verb + adverb particle (*on*, *in*, *off*, *up*, etc.). The verb + adverb particle combine to give meaning and the meaning of the phrasal verb is often very different from the meaning of the verb and the particle taken separately. For more about the meaning of phrasal verbs ▶ 100.

> The machine **broke down**. (= stopped working.)
>
> He **made** the story **up**. (= invented)

For a list of common phrasal verbs and their meanings ▶ pages 347, 350.

### Intransitive phrasal verbs

B Some phrasal verbs are intransitive (they do not take an object).

> We **set off** at 9.30.
>
> Where **did** you **grow up**?
>
> Can you **speak up** a little?
>
> NOT ~~We set off the journey at 9.30.~~
>
> NOT ~~We set the journey off ... .~~

### Transitive phrasal verbs

C Some phrasal verbs are transitive (they must take an object). The object commonly goes between the verb and the adverb particle.

> Turn **the TV** off.
>
> Turn **it** off.
>
> I threw **those magazines** away.
>
> I threw **them** away.

If the object is a noun, it can also go
after the adverb particle.

*Turn off **the TV**.*

*I threw away **those magazines**.*

However, if the object is a pronoun, it
cannot go after the particle.

NOT ~~Turn off it.~~

NOT ~~I threw away them.~~

When the object is a long phrase, we
usually put it after the adverb particle.

*I threw away **those magazines that
Jenny brought with her the other day**.*

NOT ~~I threw those magazines that
Jenny brought with her the other
day away.~~

D  Note that there are a few exceptions
to the rules above. With a very few
transitive phrasal verbs, we cannot put
the object after the adverb particle.

*I'll **call** Sam **back**.*

NOT ~~I'll call back Sam.~~

*I can't **tell** the twins **apart**.*

NOT ~~I can't tell apart the twins.~~

---

**TIP**

There are some useful phrasal verbs
with *be*.

*Tom**'s away** at the moment.* (= is not
here)

*Will you **be in** at around 6.30 this
evening?* (= be at home)

*Is that the time? I must **be off**.* (= leave)

*When**'s** the film **over**?* (= be finished)

# 100 Phrasal verbs (2)

**A** The meaning of some phrasal verbs is easy to understand if we know the meaning of the verb and the adverb particle.

*Can you **switch** the light **on**?*
***Turn** the car **round** and **go back** into town.*

However, the meaning of the phrasal verb is often very different from the meaning of the verb and the particle taken separately. The meaning is often idiomatic.

*He **made** the story **up**.* (= He invented the story.)
*Sales really **took off**.* (= Sales grew rapidly.)
*They **turned down** my offer.* (= They rejected my offer.)

**B** Some adverb particles have the same or similar meaning when they are used in different phrasal verbs. For example *up* often means 'totally' or 'completely'.

*I've **used up** all the milk.*
*Can you **tidy up** your room?*
*First, you need to **cut up** the potato.*

*Up* can also add the sense 'increase' or 'improve'.

*I need to **brush up** my English.*
*We spent months **doing up** the house.*
*I see petrol **has gone up** again.*

If we know these meanings, it will help us to understand the meaning of phrasal verbs. For a list of common meanings of adverb particles in phrasal verbs ▶ page 354.

C  Sometimes a phrasal verb has different meanings.

*Would you mind **taking** your shoes **off**?* (= removing your shoes)
*The plane finally **took off** five hours late.* (= left the ground)
*They **took** 10% **off** the price.* (= reduced the price by 10%)
*After the advertising campaign, sales **took off**.* (= grew rapidly)

*I **turned up** the volume.* (= increased the volume)
*Only three people **turned up** for the meeting.* (= arrived/attended)

*The bus **broke down** on the way to the airport.* (= stopped working / failed mechanically)
*To learn the song, **break** it **down** into its various parts.* (= separate it or analyse it)

Note also that some phrasal verbs can be both transitive (e.g. *take off your shoes*) and intransitive (e.g. *the plane took off*).

## 100

**D** Some single-word verbs have the same or similar meaning to phrasal verbs and we can sometimes use either. There is very often, however, a difference in usage and register, the phrasal verb often being more informal.

*Did you **find out** / **discover** what happened?*

*They've **put off** / **postponed** the meeting until next week.*

*We need to **fix up** / **arrange** a meeting.*

***Throw away** / **Discard** the empty packaging.*

*I'll **sort out** / **resolve** the problem.*

Some phrasal verbs, however, do not have a single-word equivalent and we use the phrasal verb in all contexts, including formal ones.

*He was born and **brought up** in Hawaii.*

*Can you **drop** me **off** at the hotel?*

*I can't **do without** my morning coffee.*

---

**TIP**

When you see or hear an unfamiliar phrasal verb, first try to work out the meaning from the context. It is then always a good idea to check the meaning and use in a dictionary.

# 101 Prepositional verbs (1)

A  A prepositional verb consists of a verb + preposition. This unit deals with prepositional verbs which are similar to phrasal verbs (▶ 99, 100) in that the meaning is often very different from the meaning of the verb and the preposition taken separately. The meaning is often idiomatic.

*I **ran into** Elena in town this morning.*
(= I met Elena by chance in town this morning.)

For a list of common idiomatic prepositional verbs and their meanings ▶ page 356.

B  All prepositional verbs are transitive (they must take an object). The object always goes <u>after</u> the preposition.
*Look after **the children**.*
*Look after **them**.*
NOT *Look the children after.*
NOT *Look them after.*

C  When a prepositional verb is followed by a verb, we use the gerund.
*I'll **look into hiring** a venue for the party.*

D  Even though prepositional verbs are transitive and have an object, we can use only a few of them in the passive.

For example, we can use *deal with* in the passive, but we can't use *run into* in the passive.

We **are dealing with** the situation.
The situation **is being dealt with**.
NOT ~~Elena was run into in town this morning.~~

**E** As with phrasal verbs, single-word verbs or short phrases can be used as alternatives to some prepositional verbs. There is very often, however, a difference in usage and register, the prepositional verb often being more informal.

The police **are looking into** / **investigating** the allegations.
I'm just **getting over** / **recovering** from the flu.

Some prepositional verbs, however, do not have a single-word equivalent.

Our customer services department **deals with** complaints.

---

**TIP**

When you see or hear an unfamiliar multi-part verb followed by an object (e.g. *deal with a problem, sort out a problem*), it is not always clear whether it is a prepositional verb or a transitive phrasal verb. The important thing is to understand the meaning. You can always check the form and the grammar later.

# 102 Prepositional verbs (2)

A  Some verbs are used with a particular preposition (e.g. *depend on, listen to*). The meaning is usually easy to understand from the verb + preposition combination.

*It **depends on** the weather.*
*What are you **listening to**?*
*We**'re waiting for** Christina.*
*I need to **concentrate on** my work.*
*Who does this **belong to**?*

B  It is important to notice which preposition we use with which verb and to try to remember this as one item, or chunk, of language; for example: *believe in, belong to, concentrate on, depend on, listen to, wait for.*

For a list of common verb + preposition combinations ▸ page 357.

C  Some verbs combine with different prepositions with different meaning. For example:

*Did you **hear about** Jenny's wedding?*
*Have you **heard of** a band called 'Gentle Giant'?*
*We **complained to** the manager.*
*We **complained about** the poor service.*
*Did Erica **apologize to** you?*

*Did* she **apologize for** being late?
You're quiet! What **are** you **thinking about**?
We're **thinking of** going to Thailand on holiday this year?

D  We use *write to*, but we do not use a preposition with the verbs *telephone*, *call*, *ring*, *fax*, *email*, and *text*.
   I **wrote to** my MP.
   **Have** you **emailed** Boris yet?
   I'll **text** you this evening.
   Can you **call** me tomorrow?
   NOT ~~Have you emailed to Boris yet?~~

E  We use *about* after many verbs expressing speech or thought, to refer to the topic being discussed. These include: *ask, complain, decide, inform, remind, speak, talk, think, warn, wonder, write.*
   They'll **talk about** football for hours.
   What **did** you **decide about** the conference?
   **Did** you **ask about** train times?
   I **was wondering about** a date for the next meeting.

   However, we do not use *about* with *consider, discuss, demand,* and *remember.*
   **Did** you **discuss** the travel arrangements?

NOT ~~Did you discuss about the travel arrangements?~~

F Some verbs require an object before the preposition.
> Thanks for **reminding me about** the meeting.
> I **borrowed €50 from** Catherine.
> **Have** you **invited Nina to** the party?
> You need to **do something about** your hair!
> Can you **translate this into** Chinese?
> NOT ~~Thanks for reminding about the meeting.~~

For a list of common verb + object + preposition combinations ▶ page 358.

G When a prepositional verb is followed by another verb, we use the gerund.
> I'**m thinking of getting** a new car.
> I'd like to **thank** everyone **for being** so patient.

---

**TIP**

We can use *depend* with or without *on* when it is followed by a question word.
It **depends how much** it costs.
It **depends on how much** it costs.

---

## 103

# 103 Phrasal-prepositional verbs

A  A phrasal-prepositional verb is a verb + adverb + preposition (*on*, *up*, *with*, *to*, etc.). The verb and the particles combine to give meaning, and the meaning of the phrasal-prepositional verb is not the same as the independent meanings of the verb and the particles.

> We need to **come up with** a plan.
> (= We need to devise a plan.)
> The printer **has run out of** ink.
> (= The printer has used all its ink.)
> How **do** you **put up with** that noise?
> (= How do you tolerate that noise?)

Phrasal-prepositional verbs are sometimes known as three-part verbs.

For a list of common phrasal-prepositional verbs and their meanings ▶ page 359.

B  All phrasal-prepositional verbs are transitive and they take an object. The object always goes <u>after</u> the preposition.

> We've **run out of** time.
> Oliver **dropped out of** university after the first year.
> I should **cut down on** the amount of fast food I eat.

NOT *We've run time out of.*
NOT *We've run out time of.*

C  Some phrasal-prepositional verbs can
   be used with no object and without
   the preposition when the object has
   already been mentioned or is known.
   This is to avoid repetition.

   *He didn't like university, so he **dropped
   out** (of university).*
   *I eat too much sugar. I need to **cut
   down** (on sugar).*
   *Our neighbours are great. We really
   **get on** (with our neighbours).*

D  As with other multi-part verbs, single-
   word verbs or short phrases can be
   used as alternatives to some phrasal-
   prepositional verbs. However, there is
   often a difference in usage or register,
   the phrasal-prepositional verb often
   being more informal.

   *I've always **looked up to** / **admired
   and respected** her.*
   *I need to **get on with** / **continue with**
   my work.*

E  When speaking, we generally put the
   stress on the adverb particle rather
   than on the preposition.

   *I'll get '**back** to you as soon as I hear
   any news.*
   *We should do **a'way** with out-of-date
   laws.*

> *I really should cut '**down** on the*
> *amount of sugar I eat.*
> NOT ~~I really should cut down '**on the**~~
> ~~amount of sugar I eat.~~

F When a phrasal-prepositional verb is
  followed by a verb, we use the gerund.
  > *Winning the cup will **make up for**
  > **finishing** third in the league.*
  > *I'm tired. I **don't feel up to going** for*
  > *a run.*

G Even though phrasal-prepositional
  verbs are transitive and have an object,
  we tend not to use them in the passive.
  > *We've **run out of** time.*
  > NOT ~~Time has been run out of.~~

---

**TIP**

*Look forward to* + noun/gerund is a
common and useful structure to say
we are thinking with pleasure about
something that is going to happen.
*I'm really **looking forward to** the party.*
*I imagine you're **looking forward to going**
on holiday, aren't you?*
*I **look forward to meeting** you.*

# 104 Verb prefixes and combining forms

A We can add a prefix or combining form to a verb to add meaning or change the meaning.

*I think David **over**reacted a little.*
*We need to **re**structure the department.*
*I was **up**graded to business class on the flight back.*
*We **mis**calculated the sales figures.*

B Some of the most common and useful prefixes and combining forms that we use with verbs include:

| Prefix / combining form | Meanings | Examples |
|---|---|---|
| *co-* | together with | *co-write, co-exist, co-own, cooperate* |
| *counter-* | against | *counter-attack, counterbalance* |
| *down-* | lesser/lower | *downgrade* |
| *fore-* | before / in front of | *forewarn, foretell* |
| *inter-* | between / from one to another | *interact, interweave* |

| | | |
|---|---|---|
| *mis-* | badly/ wrongly | *miscalculate, mistranslate, mislead, misidentify* |
| *out-* | greater/ better/ further/ longer | *outperform, outlast, outbid, outrun* |
| *over-* | more than usual / too much | *overreact, overlook, oversleep* |
| *pre-* | before | *prearrange, pre-book, prejudge, pre-register, pre-exist* |
| *re-* | again | *renew, replay, restructure, reappear, rebuild* |
| *self-* | of, to, or by yourself | *self-regulate* |
| *sub-* | under/below | *subcontract, subdivide* |
| *trans-* | into another place or state | *transform, transplant* |
| *under-* | not enough | *underpay, underachieve, undervalue* |

| | | |
|---|---|---|
| *up-* | greater/ higher | *update, upgrade, upscale* |
| *with-* | against | *withstand, withhold* |

C When used with verbs, the prefixes *de-*, *dis-*, and *un-* all have the meaning 'the opposite of' or indicate reversal or removal.

*The theory was **dis**proved.*
*The euro has been **de**valued on a number of occasions.*
*Don't **un**fasten your seatbelt until the sign goes off.*

There are no exact rules about which words take which of these prefixes, so you have to learn them individually. Here are some common examples:

| Prefix | Examples |
|---|---|
| *de-* | *devalue, deselect, de-emphasize, deform, destabilize, detach, dehydrate* |
| *dis-* | *disprove, disappear, disallow, disarm, disconnect, discontinue, disinfect, disqualify* |
| *un-* | *unzip, undo, untie, unfasten, undress, unlock, untangle, unpack, uncover* |

The prefix *dis-* can also mean 'not': *dislike, disagree.*

**D** Some prefixes turn nouns and adjectives into verbs.

*We were **be**friended by a stray cat on holiday.*
*I can't believe it. Jack has **de**friended me!*
*I need to **de**-ice the car windscreen.*
*Can you **en**large the document by about 50%?*

Some of the most common and useful prefixes that we use to form verbs include:

| Prefix | Meanings | Example |
|--------|----------|---------|
| *be-* | make or treat somebody/ something as | *befriend, bewitch, belittle, becalm* |
| *de-* | do the opposite of / remove | *defriend, debug, defrost, de-ice, defuse* |
| *em-/ en-* | cause to be / give the specified quality | *empower, endanger, enlarge, enrage* |

---

**TIP**

There are no clear or fixed rules about when you use a hyphen. Notice how words are formed when you see them and use a dictionary. Sometimes you may see the same word both with and without a hyphen (e.g. *cooperate/ co-operate, rebuild/re-build*).

# 105 Verb suffixes (1)

A suffix changes the word class of a word.
This unit looks at forming verbs from
nouns and adjectives.

A  We can form verbs by adding certain
suffixes to nouns and adjectives.
*special* → *specialize*
*short* → *shorten*
*length* → *lengthen*

Note that there is sometimes a change
in the spelling, such as the dropping
of a letter, the doubling of a letter, or
the changing of some letters ▶ page 331.
*simple* → *simplify*
*complex* → *complicate*

B  We add *-ize* or *-ise* to nouns and
adjectives to mean 'become, make,
apply, or treat in the way mentioned'.
Examples include: *characterize,
equalize, familiarize, industrialize,
legalize, modernize, privatize,
standardize, symbolize, visualize.*
*Many public companies were
**privatized** in the 1980s.*
*The dove **symbolizes** peace.*

In most cases, both *-ize* and *-ise* can
be used. In this book we use *-ize*.

**C** We add -*ate* to nouns and adjectives to mean 'give or add the quality or substance mentioned'. Examples include: *activate, complicate, differentiate, hyphenate, pollinate*.
*Is your surname **hyphenated**?*
*Click the link below to **activate** membership.*

**D** We add -*fy* or -*ify* to nouns and adjectives to mean 'make, become, or give the quality mentioned'. Examples include: *classify, exemplify, falsify, glorify, justify, mystify, purify, simplify*.
*We need to **simplify** the instructions.*
*Can we ever **justify** committing a crime?*

**E** We use -*en* to give the meaning 'make or become the quality mentioned'. Verbs formed in this way include: *darken, lighten, lengthen, shorten, deepen, heighten, widen, strengthen, weaken*.
*We need to **darken** the background.*
*They **are widening** their investigation.*

Note that the verb formed from *low* is *lower* and the verb for *narrow* is *narrow*.

---

**TIP**

There are no exact rules about which suffixes you can and cannot add to which words, so it is important to learn words individually.

---

# 106 Verb suffixes (2)

A suffix changes the word class of a word. This unit looks at forming nouns and adjectives from verbs.

A We can add suffixes to verbs to form adjectives and nouns.

*act* → *act**or***
*demonstrate* → *demonstrat**ion***
*argue* → *argu**ment***

Note that there is sometimes a change in the spelling, such as the dropping of a letter, the doubling of a letter, or changing some letters.

*invite* → *invi**tation***
*rob* → *rob**bery***
*repeat* → *repe**titive***
*explain* → *(in)expl**icable***
*destroy* → *destr**uctible***

B We can form nouns from verbs, for example *punish* → *punish**ment***, *include* → *inclu**sion***. The most common suffixes that we use to form nouns from verbs are:

| Suffix | Examples |
| --- | --- |
| -er/-or | *actor, advertiser, director, driver, manager* |
| -ee | *employee, trainee, interviewee* |

| | |
|---|---|
| -ant/-ent | assistant, attendant, consultant, student |
| -ance/-ancy -ence/-ency | assistance, attendance, endurance, consultancy, preference, dependence, difference, presidency |
| -tion/-sion | decision, demonstration, discussion, expansion, inclusion, production |
| -ation/-ition | alteration, competition, invitation, opposition |
| -ment | argument, development, government, punishment |
| -age | breakage, wastage, package |
| -al | denial, proposal, refusal |
| -ery/-ry | bribery, robbery, bakery |

*The company has over 200 employees.*
*Tea or coffee – do you have a preference?*
*All breakages must be paid for.*

C We can form adjectives from verbs, for example *depend* → *dependable*, *attract* → *attractive*. The meaning is 'having the quality of'. The most common suffixes that we use to form adjectives from verbs are:

| Suffix | Examples |
|---|---|
| -ent | dependent, different, excellent |
| -ive | attractive, effective, protective |

| -ative/-itive | imaginative, informative, repetitive |
| -able/-ible | avoidable, doable, enjoyable, indefensible |

*Journey time is dependent on traffic.*
*What an impressive building!*
*Stella's a very talkative person.*

D The suffix *-able* is used to add the sense that something can or must be done. *-ible* is a less common alternative. Combined with a negative prefix (*un-*, *in-*, *ir-*) it indicates that something cannot be done.
  *The penalty kick was unstoppable.*
  *Blake's reaction was totally predictable.*
  *This cake is irresistible.*

E Note the following forms, which take the root of a different word:
  *read* → **leg**ible
  *hear* → **aud**ible
  *see* → **vis**ible
  *eat* → **ed**ible
  *His handwriting is totally illegible.*

---

**TIP**

When there are two ways of spelling the same suffix, there is often no simple rule to tell us which suffix to use. It is important to learn each word individually.
*attendance / dependence*
*avoidable / accessible*

---

# 107 Narrative tenses

A narrative is a description of a past event. We can use a variety of tenses when creating a narrative.

## Basic narrative tenses

A A narrative typically uses the past simple, past continuous, and past perfect.

> I **was skiing** down that run that goes past the snow park; I'**d** just **passed** the park, and these snowboarders **cut** right in front of me; one of them literally **went** over my skis. It **was** a miracle that no one **was** hurt.

> Alexander Fleming and his team **discovered** penicillin by chance while they **were conducting** an experiment. They **were growing** bacteria in a petri dish when someone **noticed** a strange mould that **appeared** to be killing them. The bacteria **had become contaminated** with the mould because one of the research assistants **had forgotten** to replace the petri dish lid the night before.

- We normally use the past simple to tell the main events of the story.
  > … these snowboarders **cut** right in front of me; one of them literally **went** over my skis.

*Alexander Fleming and his team*
***discovered*** *penicillin quite by chance
… someone* ***noticed*** *a strange mould
that* ***appeared*** *to be killing them.*

• We often use the past continuous
in contrast with the past simple to
describe activities or situations that
were in progress when the main
events of the story happened.
*I* ***was skiing*** *down that run that goes
past the snow park …
… while they* ***were conducting*** *an
experiment.*

• We use the past perfect to refer to
an event or situation that occurred
before one of the main events of the
story or that occurred before the
story began.
*The bacteria* ***had become
contaminated*** *with the mould
because one of the research assistants*
***had forgotten*** *to replace the petri
dish lid the night before.*

## The narrative present

B  When we tell a story, we can
sometimes use present tenses to make
the story more immediate and more
vivid and to bring it to life. This is
more common with personal stories.
*I'****m sitting*** *on the train on my way
to London last week and this girl* ***sits***
*down next to me and it'****s*** *my old best*

*friend from primary school, Jilly. We*
**haven't seen** *each other for at least ten*
*years and we* **spend** *the whole journey*
*chatting about … .*

**C** We often use the narrative present
when we are telling jokes.

*I'm at my friend's house the other*
*day and she's sitting at the computer*
*and she* **puts** *in the password*
*'MickeyMouseSnowWhiteBartSimpson*
*HarryPotterVoldemortDarthVader*
*WillyWonkaBatman'. I* **ask** *her why*
*such a big password and she* **says** *'Oh,*
*the website says it has to be at least*
*eight characters long.'*

---

**TIP**

When past events have present
relevance or impact, we often use the
present perfect to introduce the story
or narrative.

**Have** you **heard** about Alex? She**'s broken**
her arm.

After introducing the story, we then
generally use the narrative tenses
outlined in A.

**Have** you **heard** about Alex? She**'s broken**
her arm.

No, I haven't. What happened?

She **was** in the supermarket yesterday
and **slipped** on something on the floor.
Someone **had dropped** some milk. And
because she **was carrying** a basket, she
**fell** awkwardly, … .

---

# 108 Ellipsis and substitution

## Ellipsis

A  Ellipsis is when we omit words to avoid repeating them and when the meaning is clear without them. There are a number of instances when we omit verbs.

B  Sometimes we omit only the verb.
*Norway won 23 medals and Sweden ~~won~~ 11.*
*I finished in four hours 20 and Sam ~~finished~~ in four hours 35.*
*If I could leave I would ~~leave~~.*
*Will anyone be waiting? ~ Jim ~~will be waiting~~, I think.*

C  When there is an auxiliary verb, we can omit the main verb and its object, complement, or adverbial.
*Have you finished? ~ Yes, I have ~~finished~~.*
*Whereas Wales hasn't got a parliament, Scotland has ~~got a parliament~~.*
*I haven't been there, but Jake has ~~been there~~.*
*I don't know where he works, do you ~~know where he works~~?*

D  Sometimes we use two or three auxiliary verbs. When all the auxiliary verbs have previously been mentioned, we can omit the second (and third) auxiliary verb.

*James might have left already.* ~
*Yes, he might.*
*They must have been delayed.* ~
*Yes, they must.*

When the auxiliary verbs have not previously been mentioned, we do not usually omit the second auxiliary verb.
*Perhaps James has left already.* ~
*Yes, he might have.*
NOT ~ *Yes, he might.*

E  To avoid repeating a to-infinitive, we can often leave out the words after *to*.
*Would you like to join us?* ~ *Thanks, I'd love to join you.*
*On the matter of resigning, the minister said he would if he had any reason to resign.*

However, for the passive we usually repeat the auxiliary verb *be* after *to*.
*I was asked to apply for the post, although I didn't expect to be.*
NOT *I was asked to apply for the post, although I didn't expect to.*

After some verbs and expressions (e.g. *try, want, (would) like, be allowed*) we can also sometimes omit *to*.
*Will you try to fix the car yourself?* ~ *Yes, I'll try.*
*We hoped to leave early, but we weren't allowed.*

**F** We can sometimes omit subject + verb phrase.

*I've been to Argentina and ~~I've been to~~ Brazil.*

*We're going to get married, but ~~we're~~ not ~~going to get married~~ just yet.*

**G** In conversation and informal writing, we can often omit a verb, or subject + verb, at the beginning of a sentence.

*~~I'm~~ Sorry about that.*

*~~Are you~~ Hungry?*

*~~Is~~ Everything OK?*

We can also omit subject + auxiliary verb.

*~~I've~~ Just been listening to Pink Floyd.*

## Substitution

**H** Substitution is when we replace words with another word or words to avoid repeating them. There are a number of instances when we replace verbs.

**I** We can replace verbs and verb phrases with a form of *do*.

*David arrived ten minutes before I **did**.* (= before I arrived)

*Most of my friends don't like opera. I **do** though.* (= I like opera though)

*I don't speak French, but my wife **does**.*

*I don't believe him. ~ I **do**.*

*Who made this mess? ~ Jack **did**.*

J We can also replace verbs and verb phrases with a form of *do* and *so*. This is usually in more formal contexts.

*He promised he'd call this afternoon, but he hasn't **done so** yet.* (= he hasn't called yet)

*Playing sports is good for you. The benefits of **doing so** are obvious.*

*We'll get married one day, but we're not going to **do so** just yet.*

*He hopes to climb Everest. To **do so** would be amazing.*

Note that we use *do* + *so* only for voluntary or deliberate actions and when referring to the same subject as previously mentioned.

NOT *I didn't have an exam, but all my friends did so.*

K We can replace a finite clause with *so*. This occurs with *if* and verbs such as *think*, *hope*, and *expect*.

*Do you need a lift? **If so**, wait for me.* (= If you need a lift, wait for me).

*Are we going by train? ~ I **expect so**.*

*Will he be there to meet you? ~ I **hope so**.*

*Is it going to rain? ~ I **don't think so**.*

Note that the negative of *hope* is *hope not*.

*Is it going to rain? ~ I **hope not**.*

NOT *I don't hope so.*

It is also possible to say *I think not* and *I expect not*, etc.

> *Is Alex coming with us?* ~ *I **don't think so** / I **think not**.*

L The phrases *so do I*, *neither am I*, etc. are examples of substitution.

> *I love Paris.* ~ ***So do I.*** (= I also love Paris.)
> *We're going home.* ~ ***So are we.***
> *I don't understand.* ~ ***Neither do I.***

---

### TIP

News headlines often use ellipsis, especially the omission of subjects and auxiliary verbs. This is to make the headlines as short as possible.
*Ten injured in motorway crash.*
*Stolen Van Gogh discovered in park.*
*NASA to launch manned Mars mission.*

---

# 109 Using verb forms for tact and diplomacy

**A** We can use certain verbs, verb forms, and verb patterns to make what we say or write more tactful and diplomatic. This can be useful in more formal contexts such as business, as well as in everyday situations.

### *Would, might, seem,* and *be able to*

**B** We can use *would* as an alternative to the present simple. By introducing an element of hypothesis, it makes what we say sound less direct and final and more open to discussion or negotiation.

*I'd prefer to meet on Friday. ~ That **wouldn't** be possible I'm afraid.*
*What you suggest **would** appear to be contrary to policy.*

**C** We use *might* to make what we say sound more tentative and less direct.
*We were hoping you **might** reconsider.*
***Might** you be able to reschedule?*

**D** We use *seem* to make what we say sound less direct. It is often used as a diplomatic euphemism for what is obvious.

*We **seem** to have a problem here.*
*You don't **seem** to understand.*
*Everything would **seem** to be in order.*

We can often use *appear* in a similar way.

*Everything would **appear** to be in order.*

E We use *be able to*, especially the negative and question form, as an alternative to *can* or *could* to make what we say less direct and more tentative.

*We **weren't able to** reach agreement.*
*I **won't be able to** attend the meeting.*
*Would you **be able to** help?*

## Use of the past continuous

F The past continuous tense invites participation and comment in a way that the past simple does not. It suggests flexibility, and that things are still negotiable.

***We were hoping** you would have a word with Peter.*
***We were assuming** you would be happy to sign the contract today.*

Note that the present continuous generally sounds more direct than the past continuous.

***We are assuming** you are happy to sign the contract today.*

## Negative grammar + positive verb

G Using a positive verb (*like*, *understand*, etc.) with negative grammar (*don't*, *doesn't*, etc.) generally sounds more positive and diplomatic than using a negative verb (*dislike*, *misunderstand*, etc.).

I **don't** really **like** it. (I dislike it.)
*Maybe you* **didn't** *quite* **understand**.
(Maybe you misunderstood.)

Note that we often use an adverb of degree (*really*, *completely*, *quite*, etc.) in this pattern to soften what we say.

## Suggestions as questions

H Phrasing a suggestion as a negative question makes the suggestion sound more tentative and more persuasive.

**Wouldn't it be** *a good idea to contact the Paris office?*
**Don't you think** *Robert needs to be consulted on this one?*
**Shouldn't we look** *at the alternatives?*

Phrasing a suggestion as an affirmative question generally sounds less persuasive.

**Would it be** *a good idea to contact the Paris office?*
**Should we look** *at the alternatives?*

## Use of the passive for an unspecified source

I We can use a number of expressions with the passive to avoid specifying a source of information.

*We* **were led to believe that** *there are a few problems.*

It **was assumed that** you would sign
the contract today.
It **was understood that** you had
agreed to the proposal.
It **was agreed that** there would be a
5% discount.

A similar and common expression is
*I was / we were under the impression.*
**We were under the impression that**
they didn't get on too well.

### To be honest …, etc.

J   We use a number of introductory
phrases beginning with *to* to signal
and soften the ensuing message.
**To be honest**, it's not really what we
had in mind.
**To be fair**, he did warn us that it may
not be successful.
**To put it bluntly**, your offer is too low.
**To tell you the truth**, we've had these
reservations all along.

---

#### TIP

We often use a combination of the
verbs, verb forms, and verb patterns
outlined above.
**To be honest**, we **were hoping** you **would
be able to** extend the deadline a little.
**We were led to believe that** you **might** be
willing to reconsider.

# 110

# 110 Verbing

A  Verbing is the creation of a verb from a noun without making any changes to the form of the noun. It makes what we say shorter.

I hope **to get an audition** for the part.
I hope **to audition** for the part.
I'll **send** you **an email**.
I'll **email** you.

B  The conversion of nouns to verbs has been a feature of the development of the English language for hundreds of years. Ancient verbs such as *rain* and *thunder* and more recent conversions such as *access, chair, debut, highlight, host, impact, oil, pressure,* and *referee* were all originally nouns only.

Alex **highlighted** the key problems.
Can you **oil** the bike chain?
Who **chaired** the meeting?
Harris **refereed** the game very well.

C  Some recent examples of nouns being converted to verbs include:

Many children **are** not **parented** very well.
I **was conferencing** around Italy last month.
We're hoping that at least ten of our athletes **will medal**.
Ronaldo **was red carded** in the 85th minute.

**D** Today, the conversion of nouns to verbs is particularly common in the field of technology, especially in digital communication and the use of the internet. Many words which were originally nouns have very quickly become verbs.

*Can you **email** me the photos?*
***Did** you **bookmark** the site?*
*I'll **message** you this evening.*
***Text** me when you get there.*
*I can't **access** the file.*
*What's **trending** at the moment?*

Some proper nouns are also used as verbs.

*If you don't know the address, **google** it.*
*I'll **facebook** everyone about the party.*

**E** Verbs converted from nouns are all regular and the past tense and past participle have an *-ed* ending.

*I **texted** you three times!*
*I **messaged** him about the party.*
*Danny's **unfriended** me!*

---

**TIP**

We can use many parts of the body as verbs.
*The children **are eyeing** the cakes.*
*There's someone **nosing** around outside.*
*He **mouthed** something, but I couldn't tell what it was.*
*I had to **elbow** my way through the crowd.*
*I'm not going to **shoulder** the blame.*

# Glossary of grammar terms

**action verb** (or **dynamic verb**) a verb that refers to an action or activity, for example *do*, *give*, *think*, and *run*.

**active** connected with a verb whose subject is the person or thing that performs the action. In *He was driving the car*, the verb is active.

**active participle** (or **present participle**) the form of the verb that ends in *-ing* and is used with the verb *be* to form continuous tenses such as *I was running*.

**adding relative clause** (or **non-defining relative clause**) a relative clause that adds extra information about someone or something, but does not identify which one is meant, for example *who lives in London* in *John, who lives in London, is the eldest*.

**adjective** a word that describes a person or thing, for example *big*, *red*, and *clever* in *a big house*, *red socks*, and *a clever idea*.

**adverb** a word that adds more information about place, time, manner, cause, or degree to a verb, an adjective, a phrase, or another adverb.

**adverbial** a word, phrase, or clause that adds more information about an action, such as when, how, or why it happens.

**affirmative** an affirmative word or reply means 'yes' or expresses agreement.

**agent** a person or thing that does an action.

**auxiliary** (also **auxiliary verb**) a verb such as *be*, *do*, and *have* used with a main verb to show tense, etc. and to form questions and negatives.

**bare infinitive** see infinitive.

**base form** the basic form of a verb to which endings can usually be added.

**causative** a verb or statement that expresses the idea that the subject of the verb is causing something to happen, for example *have* in *I have my hair cut every six weeks*.

**clause** a group of words that includes a subject and a verb, and forms a sentence or part of a sentence. In the sentence *They often go to Italy because they love the food*, *They often go to Italy* is the main clause and *because they love the food* is a subordinate clause (or sub-clause).

**cleft sentence** a sentence that begins with an identifying word or phrase, such as *it*, *all*, *that*, *the best/worst thing* ..., and has a following clause, for example *It is you that I love* and *That is my mother you're insulting*. Cleft sentences are usually used to express emphasis.

**combining form** a form of a word that can combine with another word or another combining form to make a new word, for example *techno-* and *-phobe* in *technophobe*.

**complement** a word or phrase, especially an adjective or a noun, that is used after linking verbs such as *be* and *become*, and describes the subject of the verb.

**compound** a noun, an adjective, or a verb made of two or more words or parts of words, written as one or more words, or joined by a hyphen, for example *travel agent*, *dark-haired*, and *bathroom*.

**conditional** expressing something that must happen or be true if another thing is to happen or be true.

**conditional verb** the form of a verb that expresses a conditional action, for example *should* in *If I should die … .*

**conjunction** a word that joins words, phrases, or sentences, for example *and*, *but*, and *or*.

**continuous** (or **progressive**) connected with the form of a verb (for example *am waiting* or *is raining*) that is made from a part of *be* and the active participle. Continuous forms are used to express an action that continues or is regularly repeated over a period of time.

**contraction** see **short form**.

**determiner** a word such as *the*, *some*, *that*, and *my* that comes before a noun to show how the noun is being used.

**direct object** a noun, noun phrase, or pronoun that refers to a person or thing that is directly affected by the action of a verb.

**dynamic verb** see action verb.

**echo question** a question which asks for information to be repeated, for example *You did what?* in *I spent a thousand pounds today. ~ You did what?*

**echo tag** a short question form that is used to express interest, for example *Does she?* in *Petra lives in a remote valley. ~ Does she?*

**ellipsis** the act of leaving out a word or words from a sentence deliberately, when the meaning can be understood without them.

**empty subject** a subject that is used because a subject is necessary in the structure of a sentence, rather than to add meaning, typically *it* or *there*. In the sentences *It was snowing* and *There isn't any coffee left*, *it* and *there* are empty subjects.

**finite** a finite verb form or clause shows a particular tense, person, and number. (A non-finite verb is an infinitive, gerund, or participle.)

**first person** see person.

**full form** see short form.

**full relative clause** see shortened relative clause.

**future** (or future tense) the form of a verb that expresses what will happen after the present.

**future perfect** the form of a verb that expresses an action completed before a particular point in the future, formed in English with *will have* or *shall have* and the past participle.

**gerund** a noun in the form of the active participle of a verb (that is, ending in *-ing*), for example *travelling* in the sentence *I preferred travelling alone.*

**gerund clause** a gerund followed by an object, complement, or adverbial; a clause in which the verb is a gerund.

**if-clause** a clause beginning with *if.*

**imperative** expressing an order.

**indirect object** a noun, noun phrase, or pronoun in a sentence, used after some verbs, that refers to the person or thing that an action is done to or for. In *Give him the money, him* is the indirect object and *money* is the direct object.

**indirect question** a question in reported speech, for example *She asked where I was going.*

**indirect speech** see reported speech.

**infinitive** the basic form of a verb. It can be used by itself, for example *swim* in *She can swim* (this use is sometimes called the **bare infinitive**), or with *to* (the **to-infinitive**) as in *She likes to swim.*

**infinitive clause** an infinitive followed by an object, complement, or adverbial; a clause in which the verb is an infinitive.

**ing-form** the form of a verb ending with *-ing*, for example *reading* in *He is reading.* An ing-form can be used either as an active participle (*He's reading his new book*) or a gerund (*Reading a wide range of literature is important*).

**intransitive verb** a verb that is usually used without a direct object.

**irregular verb** a verb that is not formed in the normal way.

**linking verb** a verb such as *be*, *become*, or *seem* that connects a subject with an adjective or noun (called the complement).

**main clause** see clause.

**modal** (or modal verb, modal auxiliary, modal auxiliary verb) a verb such as *can*, *may*, or *will* that is used with another verb (not a modal) to express ability, possibility, permission, intention, etc.

**multi-part verb** a verb consisting of more than one word (see phrasal verb, prepositional verb, and phrasal-prepositional verb).

**narrative** a description of events.

**negative** a word such as *no*, *not*, *never*, etc. A negative question or negative sentence contains a negative word.

**non-defining relative clause** see adding relative clause.

**non-finite verb** see finite.

**noun** a word that refers to a person (such as *Ann* or *doctor*), a place (such as *Paris* or *city*), or a thing, a quality, or an activity (such as *plant*, *sorrow*, or *tennis*).

**noun clause** a clause that functions like a noun phrase; it can be the subject (***What she did*** came as a surprise), the object (*We decided **it was a hoax***), the complement

(*The idea is **we set off at dawn***), or the object of a preposition (*I'm mulling over **whether to wear a hat***).

**noun phrase** a word or group of words in a sentence that behaves in the same way as a noun, that is as a subject, an object, a complement, or as the object of a preposition.

**number** the form of a word showing whether one or more than one person or thing is being talked about.

**object** a noun, noun phrase, or pronoun that refers to a person or thing that is affected by the action of the verb (called the **direct object**), or that the action is done to or for (called the **indirect object**).

**participial adjective** a participle that functions like an adjective, for example *winding* in *a winding lane* and *broken* in *a broken gate*.

**participle** a word formed from a verb, ending in *-ing* (the active participle) or *-ed*, *-en*, etc. (the past participle).

**participle clause** a participle followed by an object, complement, or adverbial; a clause in which the verb is a participle.

**particle** an adverb or a preposition that can combine with a verb to make a phrasal verb or prepositional verb.

**passive** connected with the form of a verb used when the subject is affected by the action of the verb, for example *He was bitten by a dog* is a passive sentence.

**passive gerund** a verb form with *being* and a passive participle (the same as a past participle), for example *being ignored* in *He hates being ignored.*

**passive infinitive** a verb form with *to be* and a passive participle, for example *to be done* in *If it is to be done at all, then it must be done well.*

**passive participle** a verb form which is the same form as the past participle, used after *be* in a passive sentence, for example *pushed* in *I was pushed along in the crowd* and *given* in *He was given an expensive gift.*

**past continuous** (or **past progressive**) the form of a verb that expresses an action that was in progress at a specific time in the past, formed with *be* and an active participle.

**past participle** the form of a verb that ends in *-ed*, *-en*, etc. and is used with *have* to form perfect tenses such as *I have eaten* and with *be* to form passives such as *it has been eaten.*

**past perfect continuous** the form of a verb that expresses an action in the past that was continuous or regularly repeated over a period of time, formed with *had been* and an active participle.

**past perfect** the form of a verb that expresses an action completed before a particular point in the past, formed with *had* and a past participle.

**past simple** the form of a verb that expresses the past, formed without an auxiliary.

**perfect** connected with the form of a verb that consists of part of the verb *have* with the past participle of the main verb, used to express actions completed by the present or a particular point in the past or future.

**perfect gerund** a gerund expressing an action completed in the past, formed with *having* and a past participle, for example *having lost* in *He denied having lost her keys.*

**perfect infinitive** an infinitive form expressing the past, formed with *to have* and a past participle, for example *to have finished* in *It would be good to have finished the report by Friday.*

**person** any of the three classes of personal pronouns. The **first person** (I/we) refers to the person(s) speaking; the **second person** (you) refers to the person(s) spoken to; the **third person** (he/she/it/they) refers to the person(s) or thing(s) spoken about.

**personal pronoun** any of the pronouns *I, you, he, she, it, we, they, me, him, her, us,* and *them.*

**phrasal verb** a verb combined with a particle to give a new meaning, for example *win over* and *break down.*

**phrasal-prepositional verb** (or **three-part verb**) a verb combined with two particles (an adverb and a preposition) to give a new meaning, for example *go in for.*

**plural** a form of a noun or verb that refers to more than one person or thing.

**possessive** a form of a noun or pronoun showing that something belongs to somebody/something, for example *my* in *That is my book* and *Jim's* in *I like Jim's shirt.*

**prefix** a letter or group of letters added to the beginning of a word to change its meaning, such as *un-* in *unhappy* and *pre-* in *preheat.*

**preposition** a word or group of words, such as *in*, *from*, *to*, *out of*, and *on behalf of*, used before a noun or pronoun to show place, position, time, or method.

**prepositional phrase** a preposition and the noun following it, for example *at night* or *after breakfast.*

**prepositional verb** a verb combined with a preposition to give a new meaning, for example *take after* and *look into.*

**present continuous** a form of a verb that expresses an action that continues for a period of time, formed with *be* and an active participle.

**present participle** see active participle.

**present perfect continuous** a form of a verb that expresses an action begun in the past that continues in the present or still has an impact in the present, formed with *has/have been* and an active participle.

**present perfect** the form of a verb that expresses an action done in a time period up to the present, formed with the present tense of *have* and the past participle of the verb, as in *I have eaten.*

**present simple** the form of a verb expressing the present tense, used without an auxiliary.

**present tense** the form of a verb that expresses an action that is happening now or at the time of speaking.

**progressive** see continuous.

**pronoun** a word that is used instead of a noun or noun phrase, for example *he, it, hers, me, them*, etc.

**question** a sentence, phrase, or word that asks for information.

**question tag** a phrase such as *isn't it?* or *don't you?* that is added to the end of a statement in order to turn it into a question or check that the statement is correct, as in *You like mushrooms, don't you?*

**question word** any of the words *what, when, where, which, who, whose, why* and *how*.

**real conditional** a Type 0 or Type 1 conditional.

**reduced relative clause** see shortened relative clause.

**regular verb** a verb that changes form in the same way as most other verbs.

**relative clause** a clause that comes after a noun and adds further information or identifies what is meant, for example *who went to see her yesterday* in *He is the man who went to see her yesterday.*

**relative pronoun** a word such as *who*, *which*, or *that* in a relative clause.

**relative** referring to an earlier noun, sentence, or part of a sentence.

**reported speech** (or **indirect speech**) a statement that reports what somebody has said but does not use their exact words.

**second person** see person.

**semi-modal** (or **semi-modal verb**) a verb that sometimes acts as an ordinary verb and sometimes as a modal verb.

**short form** (or **contraction**) a short form of words in which an apostrophe is used, for example *he's*; the full form is *he is* or *he has*.

**shortened relative clause** (or **reduced relative clause**) a relative clause in which the relative pronoun and finite verb have been omitted, for example *walking away from the house* in *Emily's the girl walking away from the house*. The full relative clause is *who is walking away from the house*.

**singular** a form of a noun or verb that refers to one person or thing.

**split infinitive** a form of the verb with *to*, with an adverb placed between *to* and the verb, as in *She seems to really like it*. Some people consider this to be bad English style.

**state verb** (or **stative verb**) a verb that refers to a state rather than an action, for example *be*, *seem*, *understand*, *like*, and *own*).

**sub-clause** see clause.

**subject** a noun, noun phrase, or pronoun

representing the person or thing that performs the action of the verb (*I* in *I sat down*), about which something is stated (*The house* in *The house is very old*), or, in a passive sentence, that is affected by the action of the verb (*The tree* in *The tree was blown down in the storm*).

**subjunctive** the form of a verb that expresses wishes, possibility, or uncertainty; a verb in this form.

**subordinate clause** see clause.

**suffix** a letter or group of letters added to the end of a word to make another word, such as *-ly* in *quickly* or *-ness* in *sadness*.

**tense** any of the forms of a verb that may be used to show the time of the action or state expressed by the verb.

**that-clause** a clause beginning with *that*.

**third person** see person.

**three-part verb** see phrasal-prepositional verb.

**to-infinitive** see infinitive.

**transitive verb** a verb that is usually used with a direct object.

**Type 0 conditional** a conditional sentence with *if* + present tense + present tense, expressing a true fact or situation, or the idea that one thing follows on from another.

**Type 1 conditional** a conditional sentence

with *if* + present tense + *will/can*, etc., expressing an open condition, or a future result or consequence.

**Type 2 conditional** a conditional sentence with *if* + past tense + *would/could*, etc., expressing something imaginary or hypothetical about the present or future.

**Type 3 conditional** a conditional sentence with *if* + past perfect + *would/could have*, etc., expressing something imaginary or hypothetical about the past.

**unreal conditional** a Type 2 or Type 3 conditional.

**verb** a word or group of words that expresses an action (such as *eat*), an event (such as *happen*) or a state (such as *exist*).

**wh-clause** a clause that begins with a question word.

**wh-question** a question that begins with *who*, *where*, *when*, *what*, *why*, or with *how*.

**yes/no question** a question to which the answer can be either *yes* or *no*, for example *Do you like dogs?*

# Appendices

# 1 Tense formation tables

## The present simple with *be* (Unit 9)

| | |
|---|---|
| *affirmative* | I **am**<br>you/we/they **are**<br>he/she/it **is** |
| *negative* | **I'm** OR **am not**<br>you/we/they **aren't** OR **'re not** OR **are not**<br>he/she/it **isn't** OR **'s not** OR **is not** |
| *question* | **am** I ...?<br>**are** you/we/they ...?<br>**is** he/she/it ...? |

## The present continuous (Unit 11)

| | |
|---|---|
| *affirmative* | **I'm** OR **am working**<br>he/she/it**/'s** OR **is working**<br>You/we/they **'re** OR **are working** |
| *negative* | **I'm** OR **am not working**<br>he/she/it/**isn't** OR **is not working**<br>You/we/they **aren't** OR **are not working** |
| *question* | **am I working?**<br>**is**/he/she/it **working?**<br>**are** you/we/they **working?** |

## The present perfect (Unit 15)

| | |
|---|---|
| *affirmative* | I/you/we/they **'ve** OR **have worked/left**<br>he/she/it **'s** OR **has worked/left** |
| *negative* | I/you/we/they **haven't** OR **have not worked/left**<br>he/she/it **hasn't** OR **has not worked/left** |
| *question* | **have** I/you/we/they **worked/left?**<br>**has** he/she/it **worked/left?** |

## The present perfect continuous
(Unit 17)

| | |
|---|---|
| *affirmative* | I/you/we/they **'ve** OR **have been working**<br>he/she/it **'s** OR **has been working** |
| *negative* | I/you/we/they **haven't** OR **have not been working**<br>he/she/it **hasn't** OR **has not been working** |
| *question* | **have** I/you/we/they **been working?**<br>**has** he/she/it **been working?** |

## *Used to* (Unit 20)

| | |
|---|---|
| *affirmative* | I **used to** play rugby. There **used to** be a shop here. |
| *negative* | I **didn't use to** love jazz. They **didn't use to** be friends. |
| *question* | Did you **use to** smoke? How **did** you **use to** get to school? |

## *Be going to* for the future (Unit 28)

| | |
|---|---|
| *affirmative* | I'm OR **am going to leave** he/she/it/ **'s** OR **is going to leave** You/we/they **'re** OR **are going to leave** |
| *negative* | I'm OR **am not going to leave** he/she/it/ **isn't** OR **is not going to leave** You/we/they **aren't** OR **are not going leave** |
| *question* | am I **going to leave?** is he/she/it/ **going to leave?** are you/we/they **going to leave?** |

## *Will* for the future (Unit 29)

| *affirmative* | 'll OR will work |
| --- | --- |
| *negative* | won't OR will not work |
| *question* | won't + subject + work? |

## Future continuous (Unit 31)

| *affirmative* | 'll be OR will be working |
| --- | --- |
| *negative* | won't be OR will not be working |
| *question* | will + subject + be working? |

## Future perfect (Unit 31)

| *affirmative* | 'll have OR will have worked/left |
| --- | --- |
| *negative* | won't have OR will not have worked/left |
| *question* | will + subject + have worked/left? |

## Future perfect continuous (Unit 31)

| *affirmative* | 'll have OR will have been working/leaving |
| --- | --- |
| *negative* | won't have OR will not have been working. |
| *question* | will + subject + have been working? |

# 2 Irregular verbs

This is a selection of commonly used irregular verbs.

| Base form | Past tense | Past participle |
|-----------|------------|-----------------|
| awake | awoke | awoken |
| beat | beat | beaten |
| become | became | become |
| bend | bent | bent |
| bet | bet | bet |
| bid | bid | bid |
| bite | bit | bitten |
| bleed | bled | bled |
| blow | blew | blown |
| broadcast | broadcast | broadcast |
| bring | brought | brought |
| burn | burnt | burnt |
| burst | burst | burst |
| buy | bought | bought |
| cost | cost | cost |
| deal | dealt | dealt |
| draw | drew | drawn |
| fall | fell | fallen |
| feel | felt | felt |
| fit | fitted, fit | fitted, fit |
| flee | fled | fled |
| forecast | forecast | forecast |
| freeze | froze | frozen |
| grow | grew | grown |
| hit | hit | hit |
| hold | held | held |
| keep | kept | kept |
| lay | laid | laid |
| lead | led | led |

| Base form | Past tense | Past participle |
|---|---|---|
| lean | leant, leaned | leant, leaned |
| leap | leapt, leaped | leapt, leaped |
| learn | learn't, learned | learnt, learned |
| leave | left | left |
| lie | lay | lain [rare] |
| make | made | made |
| mean | meant | meant |
| pay | paid | paid |
| quit | quit | quit |
| read /riːd/ | read/red/ | read/red/ |
| ride | rode | ridden |
| ring | rang | rung |
| rise | rose | risen |
| seek | sought | sought |
| shake | shook | shaken |
| shed | shed | shed |
| shine | shone | shone |
| shoot | shot | shot |
| sink | sank | sunk |
| speed | sped, speeded | sped, speeded |
| spell | spelt, spelled | spelt, spelled |
| spill | spilt, spilled | spilt, spilled |
| spread | spread | spread |
| spring | sprang | sprung |
| stick | stuck | stuck |
| sting | stung | stung |
| strike | struck | struck |
| sweep | swept | swept |
| swell | swelled | swollen |
| throw | threw | thrown |
| tread | trod | trodden |
| upset | upset | upset |
| withdraw | withdrew | withdrawn |

# 3 A guide to spelling

## A Third person -s

For the third person (*he, she, it*) of most present simple verbs we add -s.

*eat* → *eats*    *work* → *works*
*like* → *likes*    *see* → *sees*

For verbs ending in -o, -ss, -sh, -ch, and -x, we add -es.

*do* → *does*    *go* → *goes*
*miss* → *misses*    *wish* → *wishes*
*reach* → *reaches*    *mix* → *mixes*

For verbs ending with a consonant + -y, we replace the -y with -ies.

*carry* → *carries*    *try* → *tries*
*study* → *studies*

But for verbs ending with a vowel + -y, we just add -s.

*play* → *plays*    *say* → *says*

The third person of *have* is *has*.

## B Past simple -d/-ed

To make the past simple of most regular verbs we add -ed.

*work* → *worked*    *ask* → *asked*
*miss* → *missed*    *push* → *pushed*

For regular verbs ending in -e, we just add -d.

*arrive* → *arrived*    *continue* →
*continued*    *move* → *moved*

For regular verbs ending with a consonant + -y, we replace the -y with -ied.
  *carry* → *carr**ied***   *cry* → *cr**ied***
  *study* → *stud**ied***

But for regular verbs ending with a vowel + -y, we just add -ed.
  *play* → *play**ed***   *key* → *key**ed***

We sometimes double the final consonant before -ed. See D.

For irregular verbs ▶ page 329.

## C The ing-form

For most verbs we add -ing.
  *carry* → *carry**ing***   *teach* → *teach**ing***
  *play* → *play**ing***

For verbs ending in -e, we drop the -e.
  *arrive* → *arriv**ing***   *continue* →
  *continu**ing***   *make* → *mak**ing***

But for verbs ending in -ee, we just add -ing.
  *agree* → *agree**ing***   *see* → *see**ing***

For verbs ending in -ie, we replace the -ie with -ying.
  *lie* → *l**ying***   *die* → *d**ying***

We sometimes double the final consonant before -ing. See D.

## D The doubling of consonants

For one-syllable verbs that end with a consonant + vowel + consonant, we double the consonant before *-ed* or *-ing*.
  *plan* → *planned*      *stop* → *stopped*
  *get* → *getting*

But we do not double *-w*, *-x*, or *-y*.
  *show* → *showed*      *mix* → *mixed*
  *play* → *played*

For words with more than one syllable that end with a consonant + vowel + consonant, we generally double the consonant only when the final syllable is stressed.
  *pre<u>fer</u>* → *preferred*
  *be<u>gin</u>* → *beginning*  *oc<u>cur</u>* → *occurred*

If the stress is not on the final syllable, we do not double the consonant.
  *<u>of</u>fer* → *offered*    *<u>hap</u>pen* → *happened*
  *<u>op</u>en* → *opened*

An exception to this rule is that in British English we double the letter *-l*.
  *travel* → *travelled*
  *cancel* → *cancelling*

Remember, we never double when there are two consonants or two vowels together.
  *work* → *worked*   *keep* → *keeping*

## E  *-ize* or *-ise*?

In British English both spellings are
generally acceptable. In American English
the spelling is usually *-ize*. For example,

| British English | American English |
|---|---|
| *apologize* OR *apologise* | *apologize* |
| *generalize* OR *generalise* | *generalize* |
| *organize* OR *organise* | *organize* |
| *recognize* OR *recognise* | *recognize* |

# 4  Pronunciation of endings

We pronounce *-s* and *-es* as /s/ after a
voiceless sound.

*wor<u>ks</u>* /ks/    *ho<u>pes</u>* /ps/    *pu<u>ts</u>* /ts/

We pronounce *-s/-es* as /z/ after a
voiced sound.

*li<u>ves</u>* /vz/    *begi<u>ns</u>* /nz/    *sho<u>ws</u>* /əʊz/
*agr<u>ees</u>* /iːz/    *pl<u>ays</u>* /eɪz/

We pronounce *-s/-es* as /əz/ after *-ss*, *-sh*,
*-ch*, and *-x*.

*mis<u>ses</u>* /əz/    *tea<u>ches</u>* /əz/    *fi<u>xes</u>* /əz/

We pronounce *-ies* as /iːz/ or /aɪz/
*stud<u>ies</u>* /iːz/    *carr<u>ies</u>* /iːz/    *tr<u>ies</u>* /aɪz/
*repl<u>ies</u>* /aɪz/

We pronounce *-ed* as /d/ after a
voiced sound.

*li<u>ved</u>* /vd/    *sho<u>wed</u>* /əʊd/    *agr<u>eed</u>* /iːd/
*pl<u>ayed</u>* /eɪd/

We pronounce -ed as /t/ after an unvoiced sound.

*wor<u>ked</u>* /kt/   *ho<u>ped</u>* /pt/   *mi<u>ssed</u>* /st/

We pronounce -ed as /əd/ after -*t* and -*d*.

*wai<u>ted</u>* /əd/   *lan<u>ded</u>* /əd/

## 5 Short forms

### Short forms of auxiliary verbs

| Short form | Full form | Example |
|---|---|---|
| 'm | am | *I'm British.* |
| 's | is | *He's American.* |
| 're | are | *You're early.* |
| 've | have | *We've had dinner.* |
| 's | has | *He's gone home.* |
| 'll | will | *I'll see you later.* |
| 'd | had | *They'd already left when I arrived* |
| 'd | would | *I'd like a coffee.* |

- We use some of these short forms after question words:

  *Where's James?*  ('s = is)
  *What's happened?*  ('s = has)
  *Who'll be at the meeting?*  ('ll = will)
  *Who'd like a drink?*  ('d = would)

- after *that/there/here*:

  *That's David's car.* ('s = is)
  *There's been an accident.* ('s = has)
  *There'll be a bus at midnight.* ('ll = will)
  *Here's the bus.* ('s = is)

- after nouns:

  *The school's on Burton Road.* ('s = is)
  *My sister's just got married.* ('s = has)
  *The bus'll be here in a minute.* ('ll = will)

## Short forms of auxiliary verb + *not*

| Short form | Full form | Example |
|---|---|---|
| isn't | is not | *She isn't here.* |
| aren't | are not | *We aren't hungry.* |
| don't | do not | *I don't like football.* |
| doesn't | does not | *The radio doesn't work.* |
| didn't | did not | *I didn't see David yesterday.* |
| haven't | have not | *They haven't finished.* |
| hasn't | has not | *It hasn't rained for weeks.* |
| hadn't | had not | *I hadn't finished lunch when you arrived.* |
| won't | will not | *I won't be late.* |
| wouldn't | would not | *If I were you, I wouldn't do that.* |
| can't | cannot | *She can't drive.* |
| couldn't | could not | *I couldn't find an ATM.* |
| shouldn't | should not | *You shouldn't do that.* |
| mustn't | must not | *You mustn't be late.* |

Note that there are two short forms for *is not* and *are not*.

*He **isn't** here.* OR *He's **not** here.*
= *He is not here.*

*We **aren't** ready.* OR *We're **not** ready.*
= *We are not ready.*

- We use *'s* in place of *us* in the expression
  *Let's … .*
  *Let's go!*   *Let's have pizza for dinner.*

# 6 Words used with the to-infinitive

**Some common verbs followed by the to-infinitive** (Unit 51)

| | |
|---|---|
| agree | hope |
| aim | intend |
| appear | learn (how) |
| arrange | long |
| ask | manage |
| attempt | need |
| beg | offer |
| can('t) afford | plan |
| care | prepare |
| choose | pretend |
| claim | promise |
| dare | prove |
| decide | refuse |
| demand | seek |
| deserve | seem |
| desire | tend |
| expect | threaten |
| fail | volunteer |
| forget | vote |
| happen | want |
| help | wish |

## Some common verbs used with an object + the to-infinitive (Unit 51)

| | |
|---|---|
| advise | instruct |
| allow | invite |
| ask | know |
| assume | lead |
| authorize | leave |
| beg | mean |
| believe | need |
| bribe | oblige |
| cause | order |
| challenge | pay |
| choose | permit |
| command | persuade |
| compel | prove |
| consider | provoke |
| dare | remind |
| declare | request |
| discover | require |
| drive | reveal |
| enable | show |
| encourage | suppose |
| entitle | suspect |
| expect | teach (how) |
| feel | tell |
| find | tempt |
| forbid | train |
| force | trust |
| get | understand |
| help | urge |
| imagine | want |
| inspire | warn |

**Some adjectives commonly used in the pattern:** *it* **+ linking verb + adjective + to-infinitive** (Unit 53)

| | |
|---|---|
| advisable | pleasing |
| correct | possible |
| delightful | ridiculous |
| disappointing | right |
| essential | rude |
| good | shocking |
| important | silly |
| impossible | strange |
| necessary | surprising |
| nice | upsetting |
| normal | wrong |

**Some adjectives commonly used in the pattern: subject + linking verb + adjective + to-infinitive** (Unit 53)

| | |
|---|---|
| afraid | interested |
| anxious | pleased |
| ashamed | proud |
| careful | ready |
| delighted | reluctant |
| determined | right |
| difficult | safe |
| disappointed | shocked |
| eager | silly |
| easy | simple |
| free | sorry |
| glad | surprised |
| happy | upset |
| hard | willing |
| impossible | wrong |

**Some adjectives commonly used in the pattern: adjective + of + object + to-infinitive** (Unit 53)

| | |
|---|---|
| brave | (un)reasonable |
| careless | ridiculous |
| clever | rude |
| crazy | selfish |
| foolish | silly |
| generous | stupid |
| good | typical |
| idiotic | unfair |
| kind | unwise |
| mean | wrong |
| nice | |

**Some nouns commonly used with the to-infinitive** (Unit 54)

| | |
|---|---|
| ability | opportunity |
| attempt | plan |
| chance | power |
| choice | promise |
| decision | proposal |
| demand | race |
| desire | reason |
| determination | refusal |
| effort | request |
| failure | thing |
| idea | threat |
| intention | time |
| mistake | way |
| need | willingness |
| offer | wish |

**Some verbs that are commonly followed by a question word + to-infinitive** (Unit 55)

| | |
|---|---|
| ask (sb) | say |
| choose | see |
| decide | show (sb) |
| discover | talk about |
| discuss | teach (sb) |
| explain | tell (sb) |
| find out | think (about) |
| forget | understand |
| know | wonder |
| learn | work out |
| remember | worry about |

# 7 Words used with the gerund

**Common prepositional verbs that can be followed by the gerund** (Unit 61)

| | |
|---|---|
| admit to | confess to |
| (dis)agree with | cope with |
| allow for | decide against/on |
| apologize for | depend on/upon |
| (dis)approve of | dream about/of |
| begin by/with | feel like |
| believe in | fight against/for |
| benefit from | focus on |
| boast about | forget about |
| budget for | grumble about |
| care for | hear of |
| choose between | insist on |
| complain about | joke about |
| concentrate on | laugh about |

| lead to | resort to |
|---|---|
| moan about | result in |
| object to | specialize in |
| pay for | stem from |
| persist in | succeed in |
| plan on | suffer from |
| prepare for | talk about |
| protest about | think about/of |
| reckon on | use for |
| recover from | vote against/for |
| refer to | work on |
| refrain from | worry about |
| rely on | write about |

## Prepositional verbs + object used with the gerund (Unit 61)

| accuse sb of | prevent sb/sth from |
|---|---|
| arrest sb for | prohibit sb from |
| blame sb for | protect sb/sth against/from |
| charge sb for/with | praise sb for |
| congratulate sb on | prevent sb from |
| convict sb of | punish sb for |
| criticize sb for | remind sb about/of |
| discourage sb from | save sb from |
| exclude sb from | spend sth on |
| excuse sb for | stop sb from |
| forgive sb for | suspect sb of |
| help sb with | thank sb for |
| insure sb/sth against | use sth for |
| involve sb in | warn sb about/of |
| keep sb from | waste sth on |

**Common adjectives + preposition that can be followed by the gerund** (Unit 61)

## Adjectives of attitude or feeling

afraid/frightened/
  scared of
angry/annoyed/
  furious about
anxious about
ashamed of
aware of
bored of/with
certain/sure about
conscious of
content with
dependent on
disappointed in/
  with
doubtful about
enthusiastic about
excited about
fed up with
fond of
grateful for
(un)happy about

hopeful about
important for
interested in
keen on
necessary for
nervous about/of
opposed to
optimistic/
  pessimistic/
  realistic about
pleased about
proud of
ready for
serious about
sorry for/about
sure about
surprised about
thankful for
tired of/with
upset about
worried about

## Adjectives of ability

good/brilliant/
  OK/not bad/bad/
  at

(in)capable of
experienced in

## Other adjectives

different from
engaged in
equivalent to

famous/well
  known for
guilty/innocent of

| | |
|---|---|
| involved in | similar to |
| limited to | used to |
| responsible for | useful for |
| right/wrong about | |

## Common nouns + preposition that can be followed by the gerund
(Unit 61)

| | |
|---|---|
| advantage in/to | fact of |
| (dis)advantage of/to | fear of |
| | habit of |
| advice about/on | hope of |
| aim in/of | idea of |
| alternative to | importance of |
| attitude towards | information about |
| benefit from/of | |
| budget for | intention of |
| chance of | interest in |
| comparison between | memories of |
| | method of |
| connection between | pleasure in |
| | point in/of |
| cost of | possibility of |
| credit for | problem of/with |
| danger in/of | purpose in/of |
| delay in | reaction to |
| difference between | reason for |
| | risk of |
| difficulty in/with | success in |
| effect of | trouble with |
| example of | use in/of |
| experience in/of | way of |

# 8 Participles that can function as adjectives (Unit 72)

alarmed / alarming
amazed / amazing
amused / amusing
annoyed / annoying
astonished / astonishing
bored / boring
confused / confusing
depressed / depressing
disappointed / disappointing
disgusted / disgusting
embarrassed / embarrassing
excited / exciting
exhausted / exhausting
fascinated / fascinating
frightened / frightening
frustrated / frustrating
horrified / horrifying
interested / interesting
invigorated / invigorating
pleased / pleasing
puzzled / puzzling
relaxed / relaxing
satisfied / satisfying
shocked / shocking
surprised / surprising
terrified / terrifying
thrilled / thrilling
tired / tiring
worried / worrying

# 9 Expressions with *do* and *make*

## Expressions with *do* (Unit 89)

do your best
do some/an exercise
do sb a favour
do my/your, etc. homework
do nothing
do some damage
do research
do a test /an exam
do a course
do some work
do some sightseeing

## Expressions with *make* (Unit 90)

make amends
make an appointment
make the bed
make a change / changes
make a choice
make a decision
make an exception
make a comment
make a complaint
make an enquiry
make an excuse
make a point
make a correction
make a difference
make an effort
make friends
make a fuss
make an impression

make a mistake
make money
make a profit
make a loss
make a move
make an offer
make progress
make a noise
make a phone call
make a plan
make a promise
make a reservation
make a booking
make sense
make a sound
make a speech
make a start
make a suggestion
make time

## 10 Phrasal verbs

**Some common intransitive phrasal verbs (not taking an object) and their meanings** (Unit 99)

*back down* concede
*back out* not do sth you intended to do
*break down* stop functioning
*break in* forcibly enter a building
*break/split up* (of two people) end a
 relationship
*blow up* explode
*call back* call again later
*calm down* become calm
*carry on* continue

*catch on* (of a song) become popular

*check in* (at a hotel/airport) register

*cheer up* become happier

*chicken out* not do sth because of fear

*come back* return

*come on* (of a skill) improve

*come out* (of a film/book) be released or published

*come round/over* visit

*come to* regain consciousness

*come up* arise unexpectedly

*crop up* (of a problem) appear unexpectedly

*die down* (e.g. of noise) become less

*die out* become extinct

*doze/drop/nod off* fall asleep

*drag on* (e.g. of a meeting) continue for too long

*dress up* dress formally

*drink/eat up* finish a drink or food

*drop by* visit sb

*drop off* (e.g. of sales) decline

*ease off* (e.g. of rain) become less

*eat out* eat in a restaurant

*end up* arrive at a destination or result

*fall out* (of two people) stop being friends

*fill up* (e.g. of a room or container) fill to capacity

*fit in* (of a person e.g. in a workplace) be compatible with others

*get back* return

*get by* manage; cope

*get in* enter, e.g. a car

*get off* dismount, e.g. a bicycle

*get on*  mount, e.g. a bicycle

*get out*  leave, e.g. a car

*get up*  get out of bed or a chair

*give in*  submit to sb/sth

*go back*  return

*go off*  explode

*go off*  (e.g. of milk) become bad

*go on*  continue

*go out*  leave the house or a building

*grow up*  change from child to adult

*hang up*  stop a phone call

*hold out*  resist sth

*hurry up*  go faster

*keep away*  remain at a distance

*keep on*  continue

*lie down*  lie horizontally; recline

*line up*  stand in a line, e.g. outside a classroom

*log on/in*  connect to a website

*make up*  (of two people) become friends again

*meet up*  meet, when prearranged

*mess up*  make a mistake

*pass/black out*  lose consciousness; faint

*quiet(en) down*  become quieter

*save up*  save money for sth

*sell out*  sell all of sth, e.g. concert tickets

*set off*  begin a journey

*settle down*  become calm; become established

*show off*  boast; try to impress

*show up*  arrive; attend an event

*speak up*  speak louder

*stand up*  move to a standing position

*stay out*  not return home, especially late at night

*take off*  (of an aeroplane) leave the ground

*take off*  be successful

*take over*  take control

*throw up*  vomit

*turn up*  arrive; attend an event

*wake up*  wake from sleep

## Some common transitive phrasal verbs (taking an object) and their meanings (Unit 99)

*back up*  make copies, e.g. of data

*beat up*  physically assault sb

*blow up*  inflate sth, e.g. a tyre

*blow up*  cause sth to explode, e.g. a building

*break up*  cause sth to disperse, e.g. a crowd

*bring down*  cause sth to fail, e.g. the government

*bring out*  release or publish sth, e.g. a book

*bring up*  look after a child until it is an adult

*bring up*  mention a topic, e.g. in a meeting

*brush up*  practise or improve sth, e.g. a language

*burn down*  destroy sth by fire

*call back*  call sb again later

*call off*  cancel sth, e.g. a meeting

*cheer on*  support sb vocally, e.g. a sportsperson

*cheer up*  cause sb to be happier

*close/seal off* close and isolate an area, e.g. a crime scene

*cross out* eliminate or erase sth, e.g. on a list

*dig up* remove sth from the ground, e.g. garden weeds

*do up* renovate or improve a room or building

*drag out* make sth longer than necessary, e.g. a negotiation

*draw up* formally prepare sth, e.g. a contract

*drop off* unload or deliver sth/sb, e.g. a package or a person

*drown out* make sth inaudible with a louder noise

*fill in/out* complete sth, e.g. a form

*fill up* fill sth to capacity, e.g. a glass

*find out* discover sth, e.g. information

*finish off* finish sth completely, e.g. an assignment

*get back* receive sth in return for sth, e.g. change

*give away* give sth for free, e.g. an old bike

*give back* return sth to sb

*give up* stop doing or using sth, e.g. smoking

*hand/give in* submit sth, e.g. a report

*hand over* give or pass sth to sb, e.g. control of sth

*hang up* put sth on a hook, e.g. a coat

*hold up* delay sth, e.g. traffic

*knock out* make sb unconscious with a blow

*leave out* omit sth, e.g. an ingredient in a recipe

*let down* disappoint sb, e.g. a friend

*line up* put people in a line or row, e.g. schoolchildren

*look over* examine sth, e.g. a car

*look up* search in a list or book for sth, e.g. a word in a dictionary

*make up* invent sth, e.g. an excuse

*make out* hear or understand sth, e.g. what sb is saying

*mess up* spoil sth

*mess up* cause problems for sb

*note down* make a brief written record of sth, e.g. a phone number

*pay off* pay all you owe of sth, e.g. a loan

*pencil in* provisionally schedule sth, e.g. a meeting

*pick up* lift sth from a surface or the floor

*pick up* collect sth/sb, e.g. in a car

*pick up* learn sth without effort, e.g. a language

*play down* make sth seem less important, e.g. bad news

*print out* print sth from a computer, e.g. a document

*put away* store or put sth in its correct place, e.g. a toy

*put down* disparage or criticize sb

*put off* postpone an arrangement or event, e.g. a meeting

*put off* deter sb

*put on* start to wear sth, e.g. a dress

*put out* extinguish sth, e.g. a fire

*put up* erect or build sth, e.g. a tent

*rip up* tear sth into pieces, e.g. a piece of paper

*see off* go with sb to a station or airport to say goodbye

*set off* activate sth, e.g. an alarm

*set up* establish or begin sth, e.g. a company

*shut down* stop sth functioning temporarily, e.g. a computer

*shut down* close sth permanently, e.g. a business

*sort out* resolve sth, e.g. a problem

*switch/turn/put on* power sth, e.g. a light or TV

*switch/turn/put off* remove power from sth, e.g. a light or TV

*take in* understand or remember sth you have read or been told

*take off* remove an item of clothing

*take off* reduce the sum of sth by a particular amount

*take on* undertake sth, e.g. extra work

*take out* take sth outside a building, e.g. the rubbish

*take up* start a new hobby or interest, e.g. the guitar

*take up* use or consume sth, e.g. time or energy

*talk into* persuade sb to do sth

*throw away* discard sth, e.g. packaging

*tidy/clear/clean up* tidy, clear, or clean sth, e.g. a room

*try on* wear sth for a short time to see if it fits

*try out* test sth, e.g. before you buy it

*turn down*  reject sth, e.g. a proposal

*turn down*  decrease the volume of sth

*turn up*  increase the volume of sth

*use up*  use sth completely, e.g. a carton of milk

*wake up*  awaken sb

*water down*  dilute sth or make sth weaker, e.g. a problem, a drink

*work out*  resolve or solve sth, e.g. a solution

*write down*  make a written record of sth

## Common meanings of adverb particles in phrasal verbs (Unit 100)

### down

= moving downwards (e.g. *fall down, put down, burn down*)

= decreasing (e.g. *cut down, turn down, water down*)

= stopping completely (e.g. *break down, close down, shut down*)

= on paper (e.g. *write down, note down, copy down*)

### up

= moving upwards/forwards (e.g. *get up, hang up, dig up*)

= increasing/improving (e.g. *speak up, do up, dress up*)

= completing (e.g. *drink up, use up, give up*)

= starting/creating (e.g. *set up, draw up, crop up*)

### off

= starting/departing (e.g. *set off, get off, kick off*)

= stopping/completing (e.g. *call off, put off, finish off*)

= disconnecting/separating (e.g. *switch off, cut off, close off*)

= removing (e.g. *cross off, take off, dust off*)

= decreasing (e.g. *fall off, ease off, cool off*)

### on

= starting/connecting (e.g. *switch on, log on, be on*)

= continuing (e.g. *carry on, move on, keep on*)

= wearing (e.g. *put on, try on, have on*)

### out

= removing/excluding (e.g. *cross out, wipe out, drop out*)

= completing/ending (e.g. *wear out, sort out, die out*)

= distributing (e.g. *hand out, share out, bring out*)

= producing sound (e.g. *shout out, read out, let out*)

= identifying (e.g. *check out, point out, pick out*)

= moving outside (e.g. *go out, break out, eat out*)

= extending (e.g. *hold out, drag out, fan out*)

### in

= moving inwards (e.g. *take in, hand in, give in*)

= arriving/entering (e.g. *log in, drop in, check in*)

= at home (e.g. *stay in, be in, come in*)

= incorporating (e.g. *mix in, fit in, pencil in*)

### over

= checking/reflecting (e.g. *check over, go over, look over*)

= transferring (e.g. *take over, change over, hand over*)

= ending (e.g. *get over, be over, blow over*)

### back

= returning (e.g. *go back, give back, get back*)

= repeating (e.g. *call back, strike back, read back*)

## 11 Prepositional verbs

**Some common idiomatic prepositional verbs and their meanings** (Unit 101)

*break into* forcibly enter a building

*bump into* meet sb by chance, e.g. an old friend

*carry out* undertake sth, e.g. a task

*come across* find sth by chance, e.g. an old photo

*come into* acquire or receive sth, e.g. an inheritance

*count on* rely on sb, e.g. a friend

*deal with* resolve or manage sth, e.g. a problem

*do without* exist or manage without sth

*flick through* look briefly at sth, e.g. a book

*get in/into* enter sth, e.g. a car
*get off* dismount from sth, e.g. a bicycle
*get on* mount sth, e.g. a bicycle
*get over* recover from sth, e.g. an illness or a disappointment
*go over* review or check sth, e.g. a report
*look after* take care of sb or sth, e.g. a child, or an object of value
*look into* investigate sth, e.g. travel plans
*take after* resemble a parent or grandparent
*run/go after* chase sth, a ball
*run into* meet sb by chance, e.g. an old friend

## Some common verb + preposition combinations (Unit 102)

| | |
|---|---|
| account for | cater for |
| add to | choose between |
| admit to | comment on |
| (dis)agree with | communicate with |
| allow for | compete with |
| apologize for/to | complain about/to |
| apply for | comply with |
| (dis)approve of | concentrate on |
| argue with/about | confess to |
| ask for | consist of |
| beg for | cooperate with |
| begin with | cope with |
| believe in | cover in/with |
| belong to | decide on/against |
| benefit from | dedicate to |
| boast about | depend on/upon |
| budget for | |
| care for | |

dream about
dream of
elaborate on
escape from
focus on
forget about
graduate from
hear about/from/
 of
hide from
hope for
insist on
interfere with
invest in
joke about
know about
laugh at/about
lead to
liaise with
listen to
live on
look/stare at
look for
meet with
object to
participate in
pay for
persist in
plan on
play for
pray for

prepare for
prohibit from
qualify for
quarrel with/
 about
react to/against
reckon on
recover from
refer to
rely on
reply to
resign from
respond to
result in
search for
see to
speak to/about
specialize in
stare at
stem from
subscribe to
suffer from
talk to/about
think about/of
travel/run/fly at
use for
vote for/against
wait for
work on
worry about
write to/about

## Some verb + preposition combinations requiring an object before the preposition (Unit 102)

accuse sb of
arrest sb for
blame sb for
blame sth on
borrow sth from
charge sb for/
 with
compare sth with
congratulate sb
 on
convict sb of
cure sb of
discourage sb
 from
distract sb from
divide sth into
do sth about
exchange sth for
exclude sb from
expel sb from
explain sth to
forgive sb for
help sb with
inform sb about
insure sth against
invest sth in

invite sb to
involve sb in
lend sth to
praise sb for
present sb with
prevent sb from
protect sb/sth
 against
provide sb with
punish sb for
remind sb of
separate sth into
save sth for
share sth with
spend sth on
split sth into
subject sb to
supply sth with
suspect sb of
tell sb about
thank sb for
translate sth into
trust sb with
warn sb about/
 against
waste sth on

# 12 Phrasal-prepositional verbs

**Some common phrasal-prepositional verbs and their meanings** (Unit 103)

*brush up on* practise or improve sth, e.g. a language

*carry on with* continue with sth

*catch up with* get up to date with sth

*check up on* check or investigate sth

*come back from* return from a place

*come down with* succumb to sth, e.g. an illness

*come up with* create or think of sth, e.g. an idea

*cut down on* reduce the amount of sth you consume or use

*do away with* ban or remove sth, e.g. a law

*drop out of* leave a course of study prematurely

*face up to* confront or accept sth

*fall back on* turn to sb/sth for support

*feel up to* feel well enough or in the right mood for sth

*get away with* escape blame for sth, e.g. a crime

*get back from* return from a place

*get back to* return to do sth

*get on with* continue doing sth

*get on with* have a good relationship with sb

*get round to* eventually do sth

*get through to*  make sb understand

*get through to*  connect with sb on the phone

*keep up with*  maintain pace with sth or sb, e.g. the latest fashion

*log on/in to*  connect to a computer or website

*look down on*  think you are better than sb

*look forward to*  anticipate sth with pleasure

*look out for*  be careful about sth; anticipate sth

*look up to*  respect sb

*make up for*  compensate for sth

*put up with*  tolerate sth or sb

*run out of*  use sth completely, e.g. ink

*stand up for*  defend or support sb or sth

*talk back to*  answer sb impolitely

*walk out on*  abandon or leave sb or sth

# Index

References are to unit numbers and sections (e.g. 65C is Unit 65, Section C), to the Glossary, or to sections within the appendices (e.g. App.9).

# Key to symbols

## Phonetic symbols

| | | | | | |
|---|---|---|---|---|---|
| iː | tea | ʊ | book | əʊ | so |
| ɪ | sit | uː | fool | aʊ | now |
| i | happy | u | actual | ɔɪ | boy |
| e | ten | ʌ | cup | ɪə | dear |
| æ | had | ɜː | bird | eə | chair |
| ɑː | car | ə | away | ʊə | sure |
| ɒ | dog | eɪ | pay | | |
| ɔː | ball | aɪ | cry | | |

| | | | | | |
|---|---|---|---|---|---|
| p | put | f | first | h | house |
| b | best | v | van | m | must |
| t | tell | θ | three | n | next |
| d | day | ð | this | ŋ | song |
| k | cat | s | sell | l | love |
| g | good | z | zoo | r | rest |
| tʃ | cheese | ʃ | ship | j | you |
| dʒ | just | ʒ | pleasure | w | will |

## Other symbols

The symbol / (forward slash) between two words or phrases means that either is possible.

We also uses slashes around phonetic symbols, e.g. *tea* /tiː/.

→ means that two things are related.

~ means that there is a change of speaker.

▶ is a reference to another section where there is more information (see page ix).

NOTES